MULLIGAN STEW

Stories and Traditions of American Hobos

BARBARA HACHA

Published by MediaMix Productions, LLC

www.mediamixpro.com

To Jim—my husband, best friend, and fellow traveler—who is always ready for a new adventure.

And to my mother, a kind lady who fed the hobos.

Mulligan Stew
Stories and Traditions of American Hobos

INTRODUCTION
ABOUT HOBOS—AND FREEDOM

My interest in hobos came about as a sidetrack, in the truest definition of the word: an auxiliary track to the main track. Trains have been part of my life since I was a little girl. My grandfather worked for the railroad, and I remember watching the switcher locomotives moving cars as we passed the freight yard on the way to visit my grandparents. Railroad tracks ran directly behind the first house I grew up in, too, and my friends and I would play near the tracks, sometimes putting pennies on the rails before a train passed by, then gleefully gathering up the smashed and misshapen coins afterward. Trains were even featured in my dreams—including one colossal nightmare about being chased by one throughout the halls and stairways of my Catholic elementary school. You can work out *that* symbolism for yourself—I'm not going to touch it with a 10-foot track rail.

My husband, Jim, and I have sought out and photographed old train stations and trestles, intrigued both by their architecture and their history. We've ridden, photographed, and filmed trains whenever we could—from the Cuyahoga Valley Scenic Railroad in Ohio, to the Oil Creek and Titusville Railroad in Pennsylvania, to the Mt. Washington Cog Railway in New Hampshire, to the Cumbres & Toltec Scenic Railroad in Chama, New Mexico, where Jim had his first experience with smashed quarters.

So you would probably not be surprised to read that when I found a DVD titled *Riding the Rails* at a garage sale, I immediately bought it and brought it home. At first glance, I thought it would be about someone's train adventures, along the lines of the PBS *Great Train Trips* series. But that was where my sidetrack began. The DVD turned out to be a documentary about teenagers who rode the rails during the Great Depression.

And much to my surprise, I learned that of the 250,000 teens who rode freights back then, many were women.

That fact became the basis of my historical novel, *Line by Line*. I pondered what life would have been like for a young woman in the 1930s who rode the rails, living the life of a hobo. So I began to investigate, exploring the Depression era and the hobo culture—and inventing a life for my main character, Maddy Skobel. Ultimately, my research would culminate in a published novel and a trip to Britt, Iowa, to meet real-life hobos.

Britt lies about two hours north of Des Moines. Its population, given in the 2010 Census, was 2,069. But on the second weekend in August, several thousand more people converge on the small town to enjoy its long-running National Hobo Convention.

Britt's 111th convention took place in 2011, and sixty-some hobos gathered in the hobo jungle on the northeast part of town. For the four official days of the convention, the hobos sang and read poetry by the campfire, honored and memorialized those among them who had "caught the Westbound" the previous years, hosted a tea for women in the town, and performed a hobo marriage ceremony. The townspeople, for their part, made giant drums of mulligan in the city park for everyone, elected the Hobo King and Queen who would reign for 2011–2012, and hosted a big parade that starred a hobo float.

When I describe the convention, people are immediately curious, and I'm peppered with questions. Who are these hobos? Do they have jobs? Are they independently wealthy? Are they homeless? Do they still hobo? Why do they do it?

There is no single answer. The hobos range from teenagers to nonagenarians; some have jobs, some do not, some are retired. Some still hobo, some hoboed in the Great Depression while looking for work. Some are "bridgers"—hobos who have ridden both steam and diesel. Some "catch out" for adventure; some do it simply for transportation. Some live at the edges of society, and others have embraced the social order enough to earn master's degrees and PhDs. To my knowledge, none are independently wealthy, at least in the traditional sense. They do, however, seem to clearly distinguish wants from needs, and that is another way to define wealth.

The idea of being a hobo appeals to most of us on some level. It stirs our wanderlust and feeds our wish to experience what it would be like to be unencumbered. "It's being free," said a bridger named Uncle Freddie. "You sleep when you want to sleep. You eat when you want to eat. You work when you want to work."

The slogan for the convention says it well: There's a Little Bit of Hobo in All of Us. That summer, I got in touch with mine, and she wants to hop a freight. If you've read this far, chances are your inner hobo is also clamoring to get out, to sample some mulligan, enjoy some music around a campfire—and, perhaps, catch out to do some traveling.

In this book, I share what I've learned about hobos and the hobo culture and give you a taste of the hobo life. In Part I, "Hobo History," you'll learn what it was like to hobo at the end of the nineteenth century and into the first decades of the twentieth. You'll learn about the inventiveness of hobos in developing signs and symbols to communicate with each other, and you'll see examples of carved nickels some talented hobos used in trade. Part II, "Hobo Traditions," takes you to the National Hobo Convention in Britt, where you can experience their traditional campfire ceremony, watch as they honor those who have passed away, observe the election and coronation of the Hobo King and Queen, and get a sense of the hobo family. In Part III, through interviews and their own writings, the hobos speak for themselves, answering the questions, "What is it like to be a hobo?" and "Who are these people?"

PART I—HOBO HISTORY

I became a tramp—well, because of the life that was in me, of the wanderlust in my blood that would not let me rest....I went on "The Road" because I couldn't keep away from it; because I hadn't the price of the railroad fare in my jeans; because I was so made that I couldn't work all my life on "one same shift"....

—Jack London, from *The Road*

ELEMENTS OF THE HOBO CULTURE

Many subcultures have developed their own ways of doing things, and the hobo community is no exception. In their conversations, for example, hobos use descriptive terms and phrases that are unfamiliar to outsiders; they also invented signs and symbols that enabled them to communicate with other hobos. Some found ways to barter their creativity by producing tramp art and carved coins they could trade for food or lodging.

Hobo and Railroad Terminology

The following list is only a sampling of hobo terms—a complete list would probably fill a small dictionary—but the definitions included here are frequently used by the hobos and can be found in the interviews, lyrics, and discussions in this book.

beat a train	Early terminology for hopping a freight. See *catch out*.
bindle	A bundle of belongings carried by hobos.
bindle stick	A walking stick carried by a hobo; sometimes it is used to attach the hobo's bindle, and sometimes used for defense.
bindle stiff	A hobo ("stiff" refers to a person).
bridger	A hobo who has ridden both steam and diesel.
bull	Railroad police.
catch out	To hop a train (usually a freight) without paying for the ride.
catch the Westbound	To die.
crumb boss	The designated cook in the hobo jungle.
double-stack	A container car.
FRED	Acronym for flashing rear-end device, a modern-day device that marks the end of the train; it takes the place of the caboose.

Frisco circle	Old hobos would throw money into a pile in the center of a circle for the purpose of buying food to go into a mulligan stew; currently, the Frisco circle is sometimes used to collect money for a hobo in need, such as for dental or medical attention.
fruit tramp	A migrant worker (hobo) who followed the fruit harvest by freight train.
gandy dancer	A hobo rail laborer or track layer.
grainer	Grain cars—constructed in such a way they have 1 or 2 holes in their steel frame that a hobo can crawl into and be out of sight and protected from the weather.
hobo	A wanderer by choice—someone who works for food or lodging; *not* interchangeable with bum. (Origins of the word are uncertain: it might be from "hoe boy," an 1800s-era term used for migrant workers who carried hoes with them and were hired by farmers for help with the harvest; or post-Civil War term from returning veterans shouting from trains: "We're HOmeward BOund —we're HOBO!")
jigger	Someone who does a "song and dance" to get a handout.
jungle	A hobo camp.
jungle up	To camp in a jungle; camp with other hobos.
knee shaker	A sit-down meal, often given on someone's back porch.
lump	A handout, usually given at someone's back door.
main stem	The main hobo street in town.
moniker	A hobo's nickname; hobos rarely travel using their given names.

mulligan	Stew made from any meat and vegetables available.
pearl diving	Washing dishes.
piggyback	A flat car that holds containers or trucks.
reefer	A refrigerator car.
ride the blinds	Riding behind the coal car or baggage car, a place where a hobo was out of sight of the engineer and other train personnel.
ride the cushions	Riding a passenger car.
ride the porch	Riding the platform on the front or rear of a grain car.
ride the rails	Riding a freight train.
ride the rods	Riding the truss supports under train cars—a very risky old-time hobo practice.
round house	A round structure built around a turntable used to move locomotives for repair or to turn them in the right direction to make up a train.
rubber tramp	A hobo who travels and lives in a motor vehicle, often an RV or van. Rubber tramps have no itinerary, staying or moving on when they choose. Also called *rubber tire tramp*.
Sallies	Salvation Army.
shack	A brakeman on the railroad.
side door Pullman	A boxcar.
stiff	A person (see *bindle stiff*).
tender	The coal car on a steam train.
tramp	A term used to refer to hobos at the turn of the twentieth century.
yeggs	Crooks.

Hobo Signs and Symbols

In addition to language, hobos also developed signs and symbols to communicate with each other. These were not meant to be understood by the casual observer, but were used to provide fellow hobos with information, warnings, and directions.

During the Great Depression, for example, a cat symbol might have been scratched into the curb in front of a house in the city where a kind lady was known to feed hobos. Or a circle with an x inside might be chalked onto a fencepost near a house where a hobo could get a "lump" or a "knee shaker." In the country, not far from the railroad tracks, a hobo might notice a sign that meant he could sleep in a nearby farmer's barn, although he might find that the farmer would insist on confiscating the hobo's cigarettes until morning, when the hobo would be safely on his way.

Sometimes hobos wrote their marks on the water towers needed to resupply the steam engines. They could communicate with each other about safe or unsafe camps and neighborhoods; mark a good road to follow; warn about barking or vicious dogs; leave their initials, a date, and the direction they were traveling so a friend could find them later; or show where there's a doctor who would provide services without charging.

Jack London, in his memoir *The Road*, written in 1907, described how hobos used these signs: "Water tanks are tramp directories. Not all in idle wantonness do tramps carve their monicas [monikers] dates, and courses. Often and often have I met hoboes earnestly inquiring if I had seen anywhere such and such a "stiff" or his monica. And more than once I have been able to give the monica of recent date, the water tank, and the direction in which he was then bound. And promptly the hobo to whom I gave the information lit out after his pal. I have met hoboes who, in trying to catch a pal, had pursued clear across the continent and back again, and were still going."

The following charts are only a sampling of some of the better-known signs and symbols.

Kindhearted Lady	Kind Woman	Woman	Housewife feeds for chores	Sit Down Feed	Food for work
Food for working	Talk religion get food	Bread	Good For a Handout	Gentleman	Wealthy
18 — I Ate	Allright (Ok)	Easy mark	Tell Pitiful Story	Work Available	Tell a Hard luck story here
Fake illness here	Anything Goes	Sleep in barn	Can sleep in barn	Good Chance to get money here	Here is the place
Help if sick	Doctor	Telephone	Poor Man	Bad tempered owner	Dishonest Man
Man with a gun	Dog	Bad Dog	Officer	Police Officer Lives Here	Judge
Nothing doing here	Doubtful	Owner Home	Owner Out	No One Home	Someone Home

Camp here	Safe Camp	Bad Water	Good Water	Catch out here	Don't Give Up
Cops Active	Cops Inactive	No Alcohol Town	Town Allows Alcohol	Railroad	Trolley
Go	At Crossroad Go This Way	Straight ahead	Turn right here	Turn left here	Good Road to follow
Stop	Unsafe Place	Get out fast	Get Out Fast	Keep away	Unsafe Area
Dangerous Neighborhood	Danger	Afraid	Don't go this way	Be Quiet	Jail (yeggs)
Chain Gang	Tramps Here	Be ready to defend yourself	Worth robbing (Yeggs)	Hoboes arrested on sight	Doctor No Charge
Beware! 4 - Dogs	Hold your tongue	Courthouse or Police station	You ll get cursed out here	Cowards! Will give to get rid of you.	You can sleep in the loft

Hobo Nickels

If you're very lucky, in your grandmother's (or great-grandmother's) jewelry box, you might find an odd-looking coin dating back to the Great Depression. If your grandparents had owned a store or a restaurant, you might even discover a treasure trove of these little gems. These little works of art, usually nickels, were carved by talented hobos who used simple tools and a lot of patience to carve new relief sculptures into the metal.

The buffalo nickel, which was first minted in 1913, was a choice medium for these artists because it had two large surfaces that could be altered and carved—the Indian head on one side and the buffalo on the other.

Creative hobos would secure these nickels onto a block of wood, using screws and washers to hold it in place. They made tiny chisels out of filed-down nails and used pocketknives and nail files to scrape and texture the metal. They might transform the Indian head into a man wearing a derby or domed hat, a bearded man, a bald-headed man with facial hair, or a clown with a circus-style collar. Then they would scrape away and smooth the ground behind the face to create a cameo.

Sometimes they worked with the reverse side, sculpting the buffalo into a "bindle stiff" (hobo) with walking stick and pack, an animal—a horse, donkey, rabbit, turtle—and rarely, a boxcar with hobos riding on the top.

When a nickel was finished, a hobo could use it as a currency that bought more than a nickel's worth of something, often trading it for a meal or a night's lodging. The value of these carvings becomes clear in a Depression-era photograph of a Baltimore restaurant signboard displaying the day's specials. A hobo who found a restaurant owner willing to trade could get a meal worth double to five times the value of his nickel.

The prices of daily specials at a Depression-era restaurant.

Two hobos are especially well-known for their carved nickels, both because of the quality and quantity of their work. Bertrand Weigand, known as "Bert," and George Washington Hughes, known as "Bo," carved nickels before and during the Great Depression. Bert sometimes signed his coins by removing the L, I, and Y from the word LIBERTY on the nickels, leaving only the letters of his name. Bert became a mentor to Bo, who was the son of a former slave and sharecropper in Mississippi. Bert taught Bo about carving coins as well as the rules of the road in hopping freights and living in hobo jungles. The two traveled together for a while, but had to go their separate ways during the Depression in order to survive.

Original hobo nickels are highly prized and highly collectible today, although authenticating them can be difficult because dishonest people have tried to pass off modern carvings as genuine hobo nickels, faking signatures, styles of carving, and the like. However, if the provenance of a nickel can be traced and if the quality and condition of the carving is excellent, it can be very valuable. The February 5,

This rare hobo nickel by "Bo" Hughes sold for a record-breaking $24,200.

2013 issue of *Numismatic News* featured a double-sided nickel by "Bo" Hughes. The buffalo side showed a man with a derby, and the reverse side had a carved boxcar with hobos riding it. At auction, it sold for a record-breaking $24,200 to Dempsey and Baxter Rare Coins, in Erie, PA.

There is also a subculture of honest modern carvers who carry on the craft today, using "good" nickels from the first three decades of the twentieth century. They do not try to pass off their work as Depression-era hobo nickels, but do their carvings as a tribute to the craft and the old hobos. Many still carve by hand, the way the old hobos did.

The coins pictured here are the work of modern carver Owen Covert. Readers can see more of his work and a showcase of hobo nickels by other carvers at www.hobonickels.org/showcase.htm.

Four carved nickels by contemporary carver Owen Covert.

TURN-OF-THE-CENTURY HOBOS

Ever since track was laid for the great locomotives to pull freight and carry people across this country, some people have been lured by the possibility of free transportation to another place—if they could make their way unnoticed and unharmed. Today, we are most familiar with the hobos of the Great Depression, but earlier in the century, others followed the rails and the steam engines for various reasons—whether to escape economic hardship, satisfy an urge for adventure, or simply to feed their wanderlust.

This section is not intended to be a comprehensive history of hobos, but to give the flavor of the hobo culture as it first developed and to present hobos in their own words. These pages retain the colorful language and spelling exactly as it was used in newspaper reporting from the late 1800s and into the first decade or so of the twentieth century—including the vibrant stacked headlines that convey the drama of the articles.

Story of the Tramp:
How Hoboes Beat Their Way on the Railroads

One Who Has Traveled Thousands of Miles Without Money, Ticket or Pass—Something About That New Product of the End of the Century Civilization

(Special Correspondence)
From *The Camden Democrat*, Feb. 20, 1897. Camden, NJ

CHICAGO, Feb. 15—I have traveled about 3,000 miles by rail without money, ticket or pass, and I have found out that after muscle and nerve, what is wanted is cheek and perseverance. When a hobo, or tramp, as the respectable world calls him, is put off a train, the first thing he does is to get on again. If you are on the front of a train as she is pulling out and get caught, slip down and catch her again in the rear as she goes by. That's the only way to make time, and the hobo likes fast traveling and to make his dates as well as any other true American.

I could have come from San Francisco to New York on something mighty close to schedule time could I have stood the strain, but you do too much traveling with every muscle on the rack to keep it up indefinitely, and besides you don't have the use of a dining car. Still, you like to get sections done in time you can brag about. Doing something to brag about is quite a feature of hobo traveling. It's a game, and playing to win helps keep up your courage. The best time I ever made was from Salt Lake to Denver, 840 miles, and I made it in 52 hours but I did not have a bite or sup during that time, and though I was comfortably ensconced all alone in the empty ice chest of a fruit car—the best place I could ever hope to get—I was finally driven out by thirst and was pretty weak and tottering when I gave up too.

On the gunwales, on the bumpers, on the blind, on top of cars and inside them—these are the choices and chances of position that are open to the hobo. The gunwales are underneath freight cars, running lengthwise, about 22 inches apart, with 1 1/2 feet of space between them and the bottom of the car. It's a good place, because you can't easily be seen and because you can get in there after the train is in motion. You lie down on the gunwales, and you have to hold on tight and brace yourself with your feet, and that is all very fine till you get tired out or go to sleep. There is nothing against it except that it is exhaustive and dangerous. More hoboes get killed falling off the gunwales than in any other way. I have seen three or four dead men myself who had ended that way. If you have to ride by day on a line that watches hard for hoboes, the gunwales is your best chance. Usually hoboes travel at night and sleep by day, but sometimes business is pressing, and they have to get out of a town or do worse. The men get very smart about swinging in under a car. They do it by catching hold of the rod that the door runs on, drawing themselves up and thrusting their legs in on the gunwales. I met a one armed hobo in Ogden who could do it to perfection. To show me how expert he was, he did it time and again, getting on and off trains going faster than an ordinary cable car.

One place that is theoretically available, but is very little used, is under the cow catcher. You can sit there, face forward, in a very cramped position, bent far over, but you are no more cramped than in many another place and no colder and no dirtier, but the trouble is your nerves simply can't stand it. Nobody's can. The roar, and the jar, and the awful way the ground rises up in front of you all the time, and the terrible swiftness of the motion, are too much for flesh and blood.

You must remember that the near you get to the ground the faster you seem to be going. Nobody rides there except as an experiment and to be able to say he did it and how far. Twelve miles was enough and to spare for me. I thought I'd never live to get to the next station when I tried it. But for a man running for his life it might be a fine chance, for railroad men don't often take the trouble to look there.

The tops of freight cars are used, but largely as a road to other places. If a train is being thoroughly searched before it pulls out, it is still possible to swing on and climb on top after it is in motion and then climb down again and maybe into an empty car, if you are in luck, or on to the bumpers. The bumpers are the iron base of the coupling machinery between the cars, and it may be less deadly cold between the cars than on top, and you are less conspicuous too. It's a very bad plan to ride with one foot on the bumper and the other on the second, for you are likely to get a jerk that will throw you off. Standing on one bumper and holding on to the rod that runs down from the brake on top is something of a strain, but many a mile is being covered in that very way this very minute.

There are dodges that best all these for comfort and with much less danger to life and limb, too, and yet they are not resorted to except under pressure, because they bring more risk of being arrested. No one is likely to arrest a man for riding on bumpers and gunwales and such. It's counted that the crime brings its own punishment. When I say under pressure, I'm thinking mainly of those roads and stretches of road that are severe in hunting the hoboes off. It is the pressure of close watching that drives the free traveler to break seals and get in loaded cars. He doesn't do it very often, but some trips are desperately hard to make except in some such way. The Panhandle road, running out of Chicago and off down to Texas, is known for the hardest road to beat in the country. Then the Southern Pacific as it crosses the desert is looked after closely.

The trainmen watch the trains like hawks, and when they put you off they stand over you and see that you stay off. That is hard luck when there is nothing but coyotes and sagebrush and blinding sand within 40 miles. The simple hobo is driven to take guileful measures to save his very life. Often he just has to break the seal of a loaded car and then trust to a brother hobo to fix up this seal—a tin affair—as well as he can.

Two men at a time will imprison themselves that way, but they won't risk doing it with a larger crowd for fear of noises that would betray them. They'll take in food and water and a candle and maybe a novel or so and be very comfortable. They must have a sharp knife, too, for when they want to get out they have to cut a hole in the side of the car and reach outside to unfasten it. Their greatest care has to be not to fall asleep and snore. Snoring is a terrible inconvenience to the free traveler. Trainmen learned to listen for snores in their own sleep, I believe.

I've traveled in an empty box car where eight or ten hoboes had stowed themselves, and I and another man with some sense have taken turns staying awake and going around with a stick to wake everybody whenever we were slowing up at a station.

There is only one road, or rather section of a road, in the United States that has practically suppressed the free use of its rolling stock. One road running into Austin has carried on its last 50 miles only two tramps in about ten years. The trainmen on that division offer a standing prize of $100 and a suit of clothes to anyone who will beat them out of a ride into Austin. Twice they have been called on to pay up, and they did it like little men. Both times the tramps had ridden in the same place—that is, in the water tank back of the engine and up to their necks in water. Now the trainmen search there, too.

—Billy Patterson

Story of a Tramp:
A Hobo Tells of His Ups and Downs
in a Reminiscent Manner

Served a Term in a Penitentiary
and Spent Much Time in County Jails in Many States

From the *Dubuque Telegraph-Herald*, March 23, 1902

Some queer characters can be found in the county jail and police courts of a city the size of Dubuque. These jail birds float about the country, and some of them have spent time in the jails of cities in every state in the union. While some of these fellows have a hard record, others are not so bad, and there is after all a sort of fraternal feeling among them. This is shown in their sympathy for each other, and almost every day in the year one or more of these sojourners calls at the editorial rooms of the Telegraph-Herald for a few exchanges which they carry down to the jail and send in to the inmates to read. This little act shows how they, in this small way, want to help a fellow prisoner. A few days ago one of these rovers called at this office for some papers, when our reporter invited him to take a seat, when a little conversation was entered into.

"What is your name and where is your home?" inquired the reporter.

The man who was 46 years of age seemed somewhat surprised at this question, and seemed to think that possibly he had fallen into a trap and was about to be held for arrest, for some crime he had committed, from which he escaped. He hesitated, and then in a confused manner remarked, "Well, what difference does it make to you anyhow?"

The reporter then remarked to the man who proved to be an ex-convict, that he merely wanted to have a chat with him, when he started out with the story of his career.

"My right name is Henry Wyrick, and I was born in Mattoon, Ill., but do not belong anywhere."

He was then asked to say something about his career, and how he came to be a roving tramp and a homeless sojourner, when after some hesitancy, making a few excuses he related his life story briefly as follows:

"I was born of honest parents down in Mattoon, Ill. My father was a plasterer by trade, and we were poor, having five children, three boys and two girls. I was the second oldest and it seems I was born to rove around as I never cared to work. When I was a boy I would not go to school, and I seemed to think that I would like to dress well, and live high and be able to do this without doing any common work. I worked in a livery stable a while in our town, but that I did not like, and then I thought I would try getting money easier, so I broke into a grocery store at home one night, but did not get any money. I was frightened the next day for fear I would be caught, but that passed off. Then I went to work on the railroad on a gravel train, and when we drew our pay I persuaded a fellow to let me carry his money home to the boarding house, as he had taken a few drinks. He did so, and I jumped a train and did not stop till I got to East St. Louis. At that place I worked awhile in a grain elevator, and at the boarding house was a peddler who had $322 in cash in his pocket, which he showed me, and that night I slipped into his room and stole it. I got over into St. Louis, but was arrested a short time afterwards at Ralla, Mo., brought back to East St. Louis, tried and sent to the penitentiary at Chester for two and a half years.

"I then drifted south to Memphis, and over to Little Rock., Ark., and afterwards went to Hot Springs, where there are at all times hundreds of persons taking treatment. Most of these men are broken down saloon-keepers or gamblers, but some of them have considerable money. I got up against it there though. I took a diamond pin from a fellow and then got out by a close shave, going back to St. Louis and up to Chicago, where I spent several years. That is about the toughest place on earth. I spent much time in jail and became so hard that I could hold a fellow up on South Clark street without any trouble. I always divided with the police, so I could get through. It's easy to stand in with them in the tough districts, but I did not make any money at this game, and I often wished I could go back and begin over, as I would not pick out any such a life as this. I never could be induced to rob houses or take the life of any one, although I have become a hard cuss, I know."

Here the reporter inquired about the life of the man in smaller places, asking him about his tramps through the country, when he continued, rather reminiscently:

"Well, I have been in Dubuque before. I was here about six years ago and got fifteen days for vagrancy and just got out."

He was then asked if he ever heard from his home, or whether he ever returned to Mattoon.

"My father and mother died a few years ago, my youngest brother is dead but the rest are living, I think, as I have not heard from them for three years. I was home for a week eleven years ago, but as I was looking tough I was not wanted around, so I left and am still drifting around. I seldom work, as I have no trade and never did work—just simply tramp around from one place to another. Occasionally in summer time I take a job as a common laborer for a short time, but in winter I spend my time in jails for vagrancy."

The reporter discovered that the fellow who told his reminiscent story was remarkably well posted on human affairs and the ways of the world, although he was very illiterate. He bears several scars on his head and neck, and evidently passed through some close places, and may be considered a fair type of the older tramps who infest the country.

THE DANGERS OF RIDING THE RAILS

Hoboing has always been a dangerous occupation. Hobos endure many hardships, such as hunger and other physical discomforts, and they risk losing limbs and even their lives. In this section, Jack London discovers a bad place to ride, a newspaper reports on a possible injury, and a hobo reports the death of his landlady's son.

Excerpt from Jack London, *The Road,* 1907.

This was a four-track railroad, and the engines took water on the fly. Hoboes had long since warned me never to ride the first blind on trains where the engines took water on the fly. And now let me explain. Between the tracks are shallow metal troughs. As the engine, at full speed, passes above, a sort of chute drops down into the trough. The result is that all the water in the trough rushes up the chute and fills the tender.

Somewhere along between Washington and Baltimore, as I sat on the platform of the blind, a fine spray began to fill the air. It did no harm. Ah, ha, thought I; it's all a bluff, this taking water on the fly being bad for the bo on the first blind. What does this little spray amount to? ...just then the tender filled up, and it hadn't reach the end of the trough. A tidal wave of water poured over the back of the tender and down upon me. I was soaked to the skin, as wet as if I had fallen overboard.

A Queer Story in Circulation

From the *Mansfield Daily Shield,* Aug. 29, 1901.

Last night about 10 o'clock a hobo fell under an Erie freight train between the S. K. tower and the Reformatory, and is supposed to have had an arm cut off.

It is said that Conductor Clark of freight train No. 82, seeing the man jump, stopped the train and told the [crew] at S. R. tower. Then news was wired to the depot office and officers hastened to the place where the man was supposed to have been injured but no traces of him were found.

It is the supposition that a fellow tramp played detective with the man who was injured, giving him a bad scare and causing him to leap from the moving train. Conductor Clark said that he saw the tramp leap from the train and that his arm was cut entirely off. He declared he saw him pick up his arm and walk over to the other side of the track.

Some are of the opinion that the tramp has become faint and is lying in some out of the way place. No traces of him were found in the vicinity of the supposed accident this morning, and therefore some doubting Thomases are disposed to consider the story a fake. But Conductor Clark appears to be convinced that a man did lose an arm last night.

Excerpt from "The Brethren of the Road"

in *The Ways of the Hobo*, by A-No. 1, 1914.

...Forever cursed be the tramp who proved himself the willing tool of the Road! Soon after Mrs. Cunningham had buried her husband and embarked in the boarding house business as a means to earn an honorable livelihood for herself and her only child, a most promising youth, a tramp, to whom in a spirit of charity she had furnished shelter during a bitterly cold night, somehow contrived to portray the Road to this son in such alluring colors, that the guileless boy, believing the scoundrel's falsehoods, ran away from his home with the rascal and quickly degenerated to the miserable level attained by his tutor—that of a confirmed vagabond.

Just as if this pitiful misfortune had not sufficiently marred the bereaved widow's joy of life, there was to come home to her the same gruesome reward for a mother's boundless devotion that had to be accepted by so many other unfortunate parents of runaway boys. Less than two years after his disappearance in company with the professional hobo, they brought the son home to his mother as a gory mass, packed haphazard into a dry goods case—the whining wheels had added a new name to the long register of waywards they had crushed ere they destroyed young Cunningham.

A-No. 1 (1872–1944), whose real name was Leon Ray Livingston, was a famous hobo who published a dozen books about his travels. He spent a year traveling with the writer Jack London and wrote about his experiences in a book titled From Coast to Coast with Jack London. *The 1973 movie* Emperor of the North, *starring Ernest Borgnine, Lee Marvin, and Keith Carradine, was loosely based on their experiences.*

Many of A-No.1's books included this warning:

To Restless Young Men and Boys
Who Read this Book, the Author, who Has Led for Over a Quarter of a Century the Pitiful and Dangerous Life of a Tramp,
gives this Well-Meant Advice:

DO NOT Jump on Moving Trains or Street Cars, even if only to ride to the next street crossing, because this might arouse the "Wanderlust," besides endangering needlessly your life and limbs.

A-No.1 Pays Visit to Attica.

World's Most Famous Tramp Has Hoboed 479,491 Miles Since 1883—Speaks 4 Languages

From *The Attica News*, Oct. 20, 1910, p.2.

On Monday, the champion tramp of the world made a brief visit in Attica. He is known as "A No. 1," and his note book in which he keeps an exact record of his wanderings showed that he had travelled 479,491 miles. He calls Cambridge Springs Pa, his home town. He was on his way to the Atlantic coast and left here in the afternoon, on a time freight. He was recently in Texas where the following account of the man and his travels appeared in a Dallas, Tex., paper:

"Have you ever seen a queer cabalistic sign, "A No. 1," with date and arrow beneath it painted on fences and barns along the railroad right of ways, or carved artistically into shanties, water tanks, etc.? If you have never seen it, watch for it and you will be surprised to notice for how many years some of these marks have been decorating those above mentioned places. It is a queer sign, yet it means that "A No. 1," the world's most famous tramp, has passed through and has left behind him this mark showing the date and direction he was journeying, This man whose only known name is this sobriquet, "A No, 1," visited The Dalles yesterday and to a Chronicle representative, who called upon him, gave some very interesting experiences of his roving life.

He is well known to all the local railroad men yet no one ever heard his story, nor that his fame rests on actual facts. It will, no doubt, be interesting to repeat the same here.

He makes his living by selling a book, "The Life and Adventures of A No. 1," written by himself. It is an illustrated book and contains some wholesome advice to boys who are not satisfied with their home. He also sells beautiful postal cards with his picture, records, and autograph on the same as souvenirs.

He has hoboed, since 1883, 476,670 miles and has spent only $7.61 on railroad fare.

He has been around the world three times. He is a linguist; speaks and writes in four languages. He has prevented 20 wrecks; wears a $40 suit of clothes and a gold watch; keeps his name a secret; does not chew, smoke, drink, swear or gamble.

How did he adopt his queer name? That is a story, too. When he first started on the road it was with an older man. The latter was attracted by the ingeniousness of the younger companion, by his bright ways, his natural aptitude for a life in box cars, and riding the rods beside the grinding wheels underneath the heavy freights where release for a moment of the bar of iron would have meant a horrible death. "Kid. you're all right," declared the older one at the end of a particularly hard journey, "you're A-No. 1." The title has since stuck and the wanderer has more than lived up to it, for if ever a hobo's life could be said to be a success, it is that of this man. He travels in overalls and jumpers, but after arriving in a town divests himself of these and appears in a neat suit. He is always clean shaven and has a very prosperous appearance.

He has a profession, which is carving potatoes and in this he has no equal. Hundreds of times he has carved faces for persons for small favors. He is also a wood carver of ability.

He has a memorandum book full of cards and letters given him by railroad officials. Several of these state that he has prevented the possible loss of human life and property by telling train operators, when beating his way, of broken car wheels or other disarrangement, thus preventing serious wrecks and disasters. He has been in four wrecks, but luckily has never been hurt.

He also has [an] autographed letter from Jack London, the author, telling of their companionship on the road together in 1894.

During his travels, "A No. 1" has learned four languages—English, German, French and Spanish. His parents were of French and German nationality, but he was born in San Francisco.

His toilet set is complete, though it takes little room to carry it. It consists of a tooth brush, soap, shaving soap, comb and a few other necessaries. His carving tools are two knives, kept sharp. Blacking and shining rags occupy a place in his traveling outfit, as does a Webster's dictionary, a rather strange book for a tramp to carry.

He was asked why he had not written his book sooner, as it is an illustrated and highly interesting story, and he stated that after 25 years of roving he had to come to the conclusion that the dangerous senseless and pitiful life he has led all these years has been wasted and that perhaps by telling his own pitiful experience he might possibly prevent others from following his steps. He said that to force a boy after he once starts to wander to stay at home is almost impossible, as the maximum, "Once a tramp, always a tramp," has been many times proved to him by actual experience as he has met many a boy of fine family and home who never knew the filth, misery and dangers a tramp comes constantly in contact with, yet cannot resist a call to wander. Had these lads read a book like his own or Jack London's or Josiah Flint's showing the pitiful, dark side of tramp life, perhaps they would never have left home and friends in exchange for a roving, restless existence. When asked why he did not stop he replied: "Do you know that the call to wander is so irresistible that often on dark rainy nights I find myself walking about railroad yards looking for a chance to move on?

"You would not believe me, yet it is a fact that I realize that my end will be the same as that of 90 per cent of all tramps—an accident. This is why I have at least provided for a decent burial. In 1894, I received $1000 cash and this beautiful medal from the Police Gazette for tramping from New York to San Francisco in 11 days and six hours and with $750 of this prize I bought a tombstone in a cemetery at Cambridge Springs, Pa. Seems strange that almost every night that silent white monument seems to beckon from yonder green hillside in my dreams, entreating me to stop my roving. This I have tried to do many times, but in vain and my epitaph which I hope will be a silent everlasting warning to others who seem to be afflicted with this strange longing to roam, very aptly called 'Wanderlust,' is simply:

"A No. 1

The Rambler.

At Rest at Last."

A No. 1 Famous Hobo, Married Romance Halts Roaming of Best Known Tramp.

HIS REAL NAME A SECRET.
Thirty Years' Tramping Around the World
At Total Expense of $7.61 Railroad Fares—Learned Four Languages, Now Prominent Citizen of Erie, Pa., Where He Settled Down.

From *Salem, NY Press* [pub. 1914–1916]

Erie, Pa.—"A No. I," the "champion hobo" of the world, has settled down and married. The wanderer who made his home from Suez to Sitka has crammed himself up in a six room apartment. The tramp who has been sleeping in boxcars for full thirty years now has a mahogany bed.

For a third of a century he drifted aimlessly from Chile to Alaska. He "rode the rods" for more than half a million miles. He saw more scenery at less overhead cost per look than any man living. In thirty years he paid only $7.61 railroad fare. But he never smokes, drinks, or gambles. His only great passion was the wanderlust. And now this hobo has forsaken the road, fallen in love and married.

One night in February, 1911, a freight train chugged into the yards at Erie, Pa. The night was cold and a stinging sleet was falling. "A No. 1" was hidden away in one of the box cars dozing. The car inspector routed him out and found that he was half frozen. He took him to his shanty and shared his midnight lunch with him. The remainder of the night "A No. 1" spent sleeping on a bunk covered with black cushions in the glare of a red hot stove. It was an unusual act of kindness for a hobo to receive. "A No. 1" vowed that he would never forget it.

Last November "A No. 1" visited Erie again, and this time he brought a present for his true friend, the car inspector. He was invited to call at the inspector's house. He accepted the invitation. Then he met the inspector's daughter, Miss Mary Abigail Trohoski, a high school graduate, twenty years of age and a finished musician.

In that one night Cupid accomplished for the roamer what "A No. 1" had been trying to do for himself for a quarter of a century.

Love was stronger than wanderlust, and they were engaged. The announcement caused consternation among the ladies of Erie. They whispered about the outrage of pretty Miss Trohoski throwing herself away on a hobo.

Some of her friends came to her with tears in their voices and pleaded with her to reconsider it. All in vain. Miss Trohoski replied that hers was not the common variety of hobo. She was right. He is the most remarkable roamer in trampdom.

"A No. 1's" history is too well known to require any detailed comment. He was away from home when he was eleven years of age and became a yeggman kid. A yeggman tramp doesn't beg; he robs; he would blackjack a man for a meal. He always has a kid to travel with him, for the child can stand outside while he is cracking a safe and give him the signal when a "copper" approaches. Besides, the kid with the appeal that his tender years makes can get food for both by begging for it, while a regular old tramp would be more likely to get jail.

The yeggman that this hobo traveled with thirty years ago called him "A No. 1" kid. The boy got his "monicker" from this: tramps never have real names. They are called "Alkali Ike" or "Box Car Bennie" or the like. Ask "A No. 1" his real name, and he will reply, "Sh—sh—just 'A No. 1.'"

He has a picture of himself and Jack London taken during their companionship on the road in 1894. "A No. 1" also possesses autographed cards from Thomas A. Edison, Luther Burbank and William H. Taft. Another card has this terse note: "I know 'A No. 1' to be O.K. Theodore Roosevelt."

"A No. 1" won a $1,000 wager once from "deadbeating" his way from New York to San Francisco in eleven days and six hours. With $750 of this he bought a tomb at Cambridge Springs, Pa., and inscribed this epitaph on it:

"A No. 1"
The Rambler
At Rest at Last

The remaining $250 he spent in rescuing boys from the hard life that has held him in its grip for many years.

Nels Anderson (1889-1986), a hobo turned sociologist, became well known for his studies of hobos and migrant workers in Chicago. In his early years, he had been an itinerant laborer, working as a mule driver. He had been put off trains by railroad bulls and learned how to "beat trains" and beg at back doors for food. He pioneered a style of sociological research he called "participatory observation," earning his master's degree at the University of Chicago. A major focus of his life's work was studying marginalized people.

Homeless and Migratory Man Under Sympathetic Microscope

Nels Anderson, Making a Study for United Charities and Juvenile Protective Society—Men Living in Chicago on 40 to 50 Cents a Day, He Says

From *The Sunday Tribune* (Providence, R. I.) July 9, 1922. p. 5.

Chicago, Ill., July 8—(By the Associated Press.)—Men are living on West Madison street on 40 and 50 cents a day, according to Nels Anderson, who is making a study of homeless and migratory men under the direction of Prof. Ernest W. Burgess of the University of Chicago for the United Charities and the Juvenile Protective Society.

Mr. Anderson became a wanderer himself as a boy, he said to-day, but happened to find work on a ranch where the family took an interest in him. At the age of 21 he entered high school. Eventually he was confronted by the problem of selecting a topic for his doctor's thesis, and finding, according to his statement, that no study had been made previously of the hobo, he began to write on that subject on the basis of his early experiences. After he had written 250 pages he felt a desire to strengthen his preparation for the task by renewed investigations. Accordingly he has been mingling with tramps as one of them at their "jungles" or summer camps, on the road, in the city streets and in jail.

"The average student who hasn't been on the road himself," said Mr. Anderson, "is apt to find himself unable to approach a tramp and get his true story. Not only are tramps chockfull of suspicion and prejudices and likely either to exaggerate or to keep still if they suspect their questioner, but they have a slang of their own.

"For example a man who works with a shovel is known in the fraternity of 'working stiff' as a 'mucker'; the man who drives a team is a 'skinner'; one who tamps ties on the railroad is a 'gandy-dancer.'

Flock to Cities

"In the winter the tramps flock to the big cities. They manage in some cases to make $50 last a long while, for they know where they can get three doughnuts and a cup of coffee for five cents and lodging for 10 cents, if in the morning they will sweep off the floor they slept on. You will find 300 men on the floor of one of the popular Chicago flop houses in the winter, though in the summer the same place will be nearly empty.

"Where are the men in the summer? Many, of course, are engaged in seasonal occupations. The idle ones are often gathered at the 'jungles,' which is an institution in Hobohemia like the fashionable club in another stratum of society. The men select for their camps a shady place near enough to town for an occasional handout and far enough from town to seem secure from the 'bulls' or constables. They build shacks of wood or roofing—tin or whatever material they find handy; I have seen very good shacks built of ripped-up oil cans.

"Last summer I tramped through Idaho, Nevada, Utah and Wyoming, covering 300 miles. I talked to some 2000 wanderers and tabulated 402 cases. I had slashed my vest to carry in index cards: only one man noticed the slashing and the slight bulges. He asked me if I was an organizer for the 'Wobblies.' I said no and that was all."

Keep Some Self-Respect

No man ever sinks too low "to retain some spark of self-respect,' according to Mr. Anderson. "I knew an elderly 'blanket stiff' of the prospector type, who refused to go to an institution for treatment though he was a victim of miner's consumption. He gave two characteristic reasons. First, he didn't want his relatives to find out about him. Second, he felt that to go to an institution would be equivalent to a surrender, and it would only be a question of time before he would give up the ghost. He declared vehemently that he could never think of going home, for he had failed to communicate with his family when he was well and had money, and he would not communicate with them after he had become ill and indigent.

"Many take to the road or the city streets because they are physically incapacitated and therefore dependent, and they feel that they are unwelcome incumbrances upon their families.

"Many are the dodges employed to get means for subsistence. One man addresses a street corner crowd, 'I am different from the rest of youse stiffs. I want to get enough for a flop to-night; I want to eat to-day, to-morrow, and the day after. I'll talk to you on any subject you choose.' Then he makes his speech and hands around the hat. Anybody can get up a crowd on West Madison street, for there are always idle men who are glad to listen."

Another man who was sympathetic to hobos was Dr. James Eads How, son of a wealthy St. Louis railroad family and graduate of Harvard. He was also known as "The Millionaire Hobo." He founded and organized the International Brotherhood Welfare Association (IBWA), a union for hobo workers, which published the Hobo News, *a street paper. He chose to live as hobo and help them by forming "hobo colleges," which provided lodging, meals, education, and socialization.*

Hobo College Specializing in Work for Knights of Highways

From *The Evening Independent*, St. Petersburg, FL., Aug. 24, 1923, p. 8.

"Hobo laborers wanted." "Hoboes wanted."

When the Easterner reads these advertisements in the help wanted columns of newspapers between Chicago and the Pacific coast he rubs his eyes in amazement. "Who on earth wants to hire tramps who have no desire to work anyway?" he asks himself, recalling the bedraggled individual of the motion pictures, brother to the porch climber, or perhaps the comic hobo of the Sunday supplement fleeing from the snapping jaws of a watchdog.

A little inquiry reveals that to the Western farmer, road construction foreman and boss lumberman, the word hobo in recent years has come to have a different meaning from that associated with the character impersonated so long by the late Nat Wills. When the Western fruit farmer or employer of migratory labor asks for hobo laborers, he expects a certain kind of worker, young and virile.

What has brought about such a change in the attitude of a large element of the population toward the migratory worker, the hobo, whose appellation once was synonymous with tramp? You can find a ready answer, any day in the week at the Hobo college, 932 Ridge avenue, Philadelphia, meeting place of the recent convergence of the International Brotherhood Welfare association.

There the visitor may be Dr. James Eads How, "the millionaire hobo," scion of a well-known St. Louis family, graduate of Harvard, Oxford, and the College of Physicians and Surgeons, and grandson of the Eads who built the first bridge across the Mississippi. There you also will find A. J. Carey, resident secretary of the Hobo Labor college. The three-story building in the old Tenderloin is dilapidated, but its floors are scrubbed until they almost glisten and its dormitory is clean and whitewashed with a neat row of cots available for the homeless. A pot of "java," always warm, is on the stove and "jungle" (hot food) is there for the hungry.

On the walls are stern admonitions against drunkenness—"Intoxication and education don't mix." There is a piano. The stage is concealed by a crimson curtain. Portraits of Lenin and Debs are on the walls. A group of hobos I engaged in an animated discussion. One is struck by their youth. Hardly a man over 35. Smooth shaven. Threadbare clothing. Some wear collars. An I.W.W. argues for "economic education" of "the slaves." A gentle voiced youth opposes with communism. A single taxer interjects "land values." The air is filled with "social control," "mass action," "the I.W.W.'s worst enemy is the boss that gives good conditions," "dictatorship of the proletariat," "ameliorists," "a real labor party for the workers."

Dr. How smiles. He takes little part in the conversation, but he is not aloof. His sympathetic eyes gaze through silver-rimmed glasses. He looks his 56 years. His face is lined and his beard gray. The son of the former vice-president of the Wabash railroad, he puts in a word here and there. His manner is unobtrusive. He speaks of the religion of human brotherhood, cooperative effort, the philosophy of Jesus, Buddha, Zoroaster. An outsider senses that he keeps his erudition in check, using familiar forms of speech. The hoboes address him as one of their own, but they are not rude nor is their manner servile. He is "comrade," "brother" or "Doc." To them is not the man whose $500,000 fortune is devoted to the welfare of the migratory worker, on whose behalf he has established half a dozen colleges.

"Lots of people think of the hobo as vile because he selects places like this Tenderloin in which to spend his winter," said Dr. How. "It is the cheap rooming houses, the cheap restaurants and the employment agencies that attract him. These men are absolutely homeless, separated from their families if they have any, and after the year's work is done they congregate in the populated sections waiting till jobs are ready for them.

"They start out in the spring, some taking the northwest course around the lakes, doing the hard labor in the big industrial centers such as Cleveland and Chicago and then, in planning time, they are found on the other side of Chicago, from Canada to the gulf. They work in the fields, operating the tractors, using their traveling kitchens and rolling up in their blankets at night, sleeping under the stars. "Blanket stiffs," they are called.

"In July and August they are in Oklahoma and the Far West, harvesting the crops, picking berries. In September and October the migratory worker is in the orange groves of California and the lumber camps of Washington and Oregon. In the fall there is the backward migration to the big cities for the winter and sources of winter employment. Some ride on the cushions and some on freights.

"The migratory worker builds the great irrigation dams. He constructs the fine roads over which the tourists travel. Many a touring party speeding over smooth highways does not know that hobo labor built those roads. The hobo stays by the job until he is forced from it. The tramp runs away from the job. The hobo runs after it, he insists on a job and on good working conditions.

"As the hobo moves on following the job, he avoids cities and camps, living outdoors in what he calls jungle fashion, like the primitive Christians. Once he was generally looked down on and despised. That is changing. He is regarded for what he is, a man with a sensible regard for his work and a man's desire for human living conditions. It is because of the misunderstandings that beset him on the road, that traps laid for him in the larger cities and the impositions forced on the homeless migratory worker that led four years ago to the establishment of the first Hobo college. We are pledged to make the good people of American understand the meaning of the word hobo. Once the ancient prophets were in bad repute. Lincoln was severely attacked because of his views on chattel slavery. The abolitionists were reviled. But persistence and struggle won. Some day the people of the United States will be glad to shake hands with the hobo worker, for they will understand what he is. That day is not far off."

WOMEN ON THE RAILS

Men were not the only ones who felt the lure of the rails. Women also rode, usually dressed in men's clothes. One of the books published in 1914 by Leon Ray Livingston, widely known as A-No. 1, was titled The Adventures of a Female Tramp. *An inside page conveyed this information:*

The Adventures of a Female Tramp
by A-No. 1, The Famous Tramp.
Written by himself from actual experiences of his own life. Absolutely moral. Highly Interesting.
1914.

Annually
in the United States and Canada
10,000
Girls and Women take to the road.
2,500
become confirmed vagabonds
OF THESE 2,000 become drunkards
500 end their days as street beggars or peddlers
400 are injured or maimed
250 are killed by tramps, exposure, trains, etc.

There are at the present time thousands of' female hoboes, many of them dressed in masculine attire, roaming about the United States and the Dominion of Canada. The newspapers daily contain articles telling of the disappearance of girls and women, many of whom sooner or later drift into the ranks of the hobo army, to lead there the miserable existence I have so vividly described in this, my fifth book.

Society seems especially uncomfortable with the idea of women hobos. As the following articles show, women were often arrested for impersonating men—and were often released when the authorities couldn't figure out what offense to charge women with.

Odd Trip of a Man and His Wife

Went Tramping Hobo Style, the Woman in a Boy's Garb—They Were Arrested 17 Times

From the *Reading Eagle*, Reading, PA, October 12, 1902, p. 5.

Chicago: Mr. and Mrs. James Smith have returned to Chicago after having been away on a trip since last May.

This may not be a very startling piece of news, but is bound to provoke inquiry. It is safe to wager that nearly everyone who reads the items will wonder, "Which Mr. and Mrs. James Smith?"

This is not the story of a millionaire and his wife going to the Pacific coast. In fact, the couple left Chicago with but a few cents in change, a small hand valise containing a marriage certificate and a few articles of feminine wearing apparel.

Mr. and Mrs. Smith did not have personal mention in the Chicago papers when they departed on their journey. They did not purchase tickets or ride in Pullman cars. The manner of their leaving was unheralded.

One dark night they crept down to the railroad yards and watched their chance. They found a freight train with its nose pointed westward.

"All right!" whispered Mr. Smith as the engineer gave two short, sharp blasts following the signal to go ahead from the conductor perched on top of the train.

Mr. Smith got under the moving train and settled himself snugly on the rods. He reached out, and Mrs. Smith was swung under and she, too, was soon securely perched there, with her husband's strong right arm holding her as in a vise.

That was the way they started from Chicago. And that was the way they came back.

After they had ridden to the end of a division they found that Mrs. Smith's skirts were a very grave drawback to that sort of travel.

"I'll dress up as a boy," said the plucky little woman.

"All right," said the husband.

They obtained some overalls, boy's size, a blue jumper, an old cap and some cast-off boy's shoes. The tawny hair was clipped close to Mrs. Smith's shapely head, and she stepped out a veritable boy.

For the next four months Mrs. Smith was known as "the kid." She passed everywhere for a boy of 17. She acquired a boyish swing in walking, and could keep up with most of the people who were beating their way westward. Mr. Smith kept close watch over his wife and saw that she was not imposed upon.

Once on their westward journey the man was called upon to suffer excruciating agony on account of his wife, but he bore it bravely without a murmur. He bears the marks of the torture on his arm to this day, and is liable to bear them to the grave.

They were riding under a freight train and the woman became faint. She would have fallen had the man not caught her in time. In catching her he was thrown in such a position that his arm came in contact with the car wheel and it ground and burned his arm frightfully and tore his clothing, but he hung grimly on until the train finally stopped and he was able to extricate himself from the terrible situation.

As they made their way westward they encountered many town marshals who looked suspiciously at the "boy." Many said it was no boy, but a woman dressed up to represent one. Several times the couple had to appear in police court, and during the round trip the man and the woman faced police judges 17 times, the woman each time being charged with impersonating a man.

They were released each time and allowed to proceed on their journey. They arrived in California finally, and got to San Francisco.

They became imbued with the idea that Honolulu would be a good place to settle down in. Mr. Smith got work on a boat, and Mrs. Smith, still passing as a boy, took a place as dishwasher. They arrived in Honolulu penniless but happy. But there they met with failure. They could not find work so they were forced to appeal to the consul, who furnished them with passage back to America. When they arrived in California it was fruit picking time. They hired out at $1.25 per day picking apricots and peaches.

They finally decided to return to Chicago, their former home. They proceeded, as in their onward journey, to "hop" trains, but were delayed many times. They were arrested and harassed. On their journey out the valise containing their marriage certificate was stolen. When they were arrested the police judges were anxious to know if the couple were married. They had no proof, and this was embarrassing.

When they arrived at Denver they decided to put a stop to the trouble, so they went to a justice of the peace and asked to be married.

The judge came near fainting when he saw Mr. Smith standing there with a boy apparently about 17 years of age asking that a marriage ceremony be performed.

"But I can't marry two men," said the judge when he finally got enough breath to speak.

"But I am a woman," spoke up the lad with the overalls, the jumper and the boy's cap.

Mr. and Mrs. Smith have the certificate with them now. It is signed by Justice Hynes of Denver.

"We have been married twice," said Mr. Smith in talking of the matter after his return. "We hope to settle down in Chicago.

"I don't know how my wife will like to settle down to keeping house, I am sure. She has worn the breeches so long I am afraid she will want to keep right on."

Mrs. Smith is 19 years of age. She is tanned as brown as any country boy, her hair is bobbed off and she looks for all the world like a wiry lad.

Skirts seem awkward to her. In fact, she acts more like a boy now than like a woman, and it remained for an Illinois town marshal to arrest her on the charge of impersonating a woman. As they neared Chicago Mr. Smith advised his wife to put on her skirts again. Reluctantly she complied.

Bride Was a Hobo

Police Arrest Couple—They Turn Out to Be Newlywed on Their Honeymoon

From *Spokane Daily Chronicle*, Aug. 3, 1910, p. 20

JOLIET, Ill. Aug. 3—Mr. and Mrs. Walter S. Jarhoe of Kansas City are occupying cells at the Joliet police station because the woman masqueraded with her husband in male attire. They have been hoboing since their marriage a month ago. Mrs. Jarhoe was formerly Jeannette Rich.

The pair shows traces of refinement. They declare their whole purpose in tramping and boarding blind baggage cars was to experience a novel honeymoon.

According to their story they hastened out of Kansas City as soon as the preacher tied the knot, and the bride donned a man's suit. They went to Denver on a freight train. Both procured places as "bell hops" in the same hotel and when the novelty of that experience wore off they beat their way to Chicago.

They visited places of amusement and spent all their money. Monday afternoon they boarded a freight train for Joliet. They were planning for another freight ride when a railroad detective discovered the effeminate maneuvers of one of the hoboes. Mrs. Jarhoe cried just a little when she and "hubby" were marched to the police station. As the iron door clanked behind them in different cells, she broke down. The pair probably will be released.

Girl Hobo Tells Story to Judge

From *The Portsmouth Daily Times*, Portsmouth, Ohio. Nov. 2, 1915, p. 11.

Behind the bars of the county jail, Eva Sampson, the "girl hobo," had time to reflect and repent Thursday night over her shabby treatment of Judge Blair, the county and city officials and the humane officer. Accordingly when she was offered a steaming breakfast Friday morning she opened up her heart to the court, so to speak. She told the judge all he wished to know and then some.

D.H. Woods was the name she gave as that of the alleged railroad employee who traveled with her in a boxcar Wednesday night. Her accusations place his home as Williamson. N & W officials of this division have failed to find such a name among the list of their employees and if he is working for the road it is not on this division. A more thorough investigation into the identity of the man is to be made.

Judge Blair learned from the Huntington police department that the "girl" is a woman in full bloom, she being 24 years of age. Her reputation in Huntington is "shady" almost unto darkness to say the least. Judge Blair is holding her in hopes of securing further evidence against the man she implicates.

At her own request she was allowed to attire in the dress of her own sex. A suit case she carried when arrested contained the necessary fluffy ruffles to transform her into a semi-respectable appearance at least.

Friday morning she became a little peeved because the sheriff refused to pay any attention to her chatterings and she endeavored to tear the door down. One attempt was enough, however, as the sheriff quickly quieted her and she was as meek as a lamb the remainder of the day.

Girl Hobo Arrested While Posing as Boy
From *The Milwaukee Sentinel*, Nov. 2, 1915

DELAVAN, Wis., Nov 2—(Special)—Masquerading as a boy, pretty, rosy cheeked Elsie McCarthy, 18 years old, was arrested here by the town marshal at the farm home of C. R. Bristol, along the Milwaukee railroad, where she asked for water and food.

When Mrs. Bristol declared she was a girl, Miss McCarthy admitted it and said she was hoboing from her home in Lansing, Mich., to join her father, Charles McCarthy, and brother on a ranch at Circle, Mont. She was detained here until Monday afternoon, when District Attorney Sumner held that she could not be charged with any offense and authorized her release. She immediately was taken in by a family and given employment.

The girl states that she "beat" her way across the lake from Lansing to Milwaukee on Saturday, and leaving there on Sunday walked direct this far, having slept in a barn on the route Saturday night. She had $10 when she left Lansing, but that was about exhausted when she was taken into custody.

RUN-INS WITH THE LAW

To be homeless and without visible means of support was considered a crime, called vagrancy, which was vigorously prosecuted in the early twentieth century. Hobos who were vagrants were often convicted without a jury hearing and could be forced to work without pay on a farm for 30 days or more. In 1972 the U.S. Supreme Court ruled that a Florida vagrancy statute was unconstitutional because it was too vague and undefined. Since then, arrests for vagrancy could be made only if they were tied to observable acts, such as panhandling.

Pinched

The following is an excerpt from Jack London's memoir, The Road, *published in 1907.*

I rode into Niagara Falls in a "side-door Pullman," or, in common parlance, a box-car. A flat-car, by the way, is known amongst the fraternity as a "gondola," with the second syllable emphasized and pronounced long. But to return. I arrived in the afternoon and headed straight from the freight train to the falls. Once my eyes were filled with that wonder-vision of down-rushing water, I was lost. I could not tear myself away long enough to "batter" the "privates" (domiciles) for my supper. Even a "set-down" could not have lured me away...

Jack London then found a place to sleep for the night and got up early, about 5 a.m. to have another look at the falls.

The town was asleep when I entered it. As I came along the quiet street, I saw three men coming toward me along the sidewalk. They were walking abreast. Hoboes, I decided, like myself, who had got up early. In this surmise I was not quite correct. I was only sixty-six and two-thirds per cent correct. The men on each side were hoboes all right, but the man in the middle wasn't. I directed my steps to the edge of the sidewalk in order to let the trio go by. But it didn't go by. At some word from the man in the centre, all three halted, and he of the centre addressed me.

I piped the lay on the instant. He was a "fly-cop" and the two hoboes were his prisoners…

"What hotel are you stopping at?" he queried.

He had me. I wasn't stopping at any hotel, and, since I did not know the name of a hotel in the place, I could not claim residence in any of them. Also, I was up too early in the morning. Everything was against me.

"I just arrived," I said.

"Well, you turn around and walk in front of me, and not too far in front. There's somebody wants to see you."

I was "pinched." I knew who wanted to see me. With that "fly-cop" and the two hoboes at my heels, and under the direction of the former, I led the way to the city jail. There we were searched and our names registered….The time was somewhere in the latter part of June, 1894. It was only a few days after my arrest that the great railroad strike began.

From the office we were led to the "Hobo" and locked in. The "Hobo" is that part of a prison where the minor offenders are confined together in a large iron cage. Since hoboes constitute the principal division of the minor offenders, the aforesaid iron cage is called the Hobo. Here we met several hoboes who had already been pinched that morning, and every little while the door was unlocked and two or three more were thrust in on us. At last, when we totalled sixteen, we were led upstairs into the courtroom.

In the court-room were the sixteen prisoners, the judge, and two bailiffs. The judge seemed to act as his own clerk. There were no witnesses. There were no citizens of Niagara Falls present to look on and see how justice was administered in their community. The judge glanced at the list of cases before him and called out a name. A hobo stood up. The judge glanced at a bailiff. "Vagrancy, your Honor," said the bailiff. "Thirty days," said his Honor. The hobo sat down, and the judge was calling another name and another hobo was rising to his feet.

The trial of that hobo had taken just about fifteen seconds. The trial of the next hobo came off with equal celerity. The bailiff said, "Vagrancy, your Honor," and his Honor said, "Thirty days." Thus it went like clockwork, fifteen seconds to a hobo—and thirty days.

They are poor dumb cattle, I thought to myself. But wait till my turn comes; I'll give his Honor a "spiel." Part way along in the performance, his Honor, moved by some whim, gave one of us an opportunity to speak. As chance would have it, this man was not a genuine hobo. He bore none of the ear-marks of the professional "stiff." Had he approached the rest of us, while waiting at a water-tank for a freight, we should have unhesitatingly classified him as a "gay-cat." Gay-cat is the synonym for tenderfoot in Hobo Land. This gay-cat was well along in years — somewhere around forty-five, I should judge. His shoulders were humped a trifle, and his face was seamed by weather-beat.

For many years, according to his story, he had driven team for some firm in (if I remember rightly) Lockport, New York. The firm had ceased to prosper, and finally, in the hard times of 1893, had gone out of business. He had been kept on to the last, though toward the last his work had been very irregular. He went on and explained at length his difficulties in getting work (when so many were out of work) during the succeeding months. In the end, deciding that he would find better opportunities for work on the Lakes, he had started for Buffalo. Of course he was "broke," and there he was. That was all.

"Thirty days," said his Honor, and called another hobo's name.

Said hobo got up. "Vagrancy, your Honor," said the bailiff, and his Honor said, "Thirty days." And so it went, fifteen seconds and thirty days to each hobo. The machine of justice was grinding smoothly. Most likely, considering how early it was in the morning, his Honor had not yet had his breakfast and was in a hurry.

But my American blood was up. Behind me were the many generations of my American ancestry. One of the kinds of liberty those ancestors of mine had fought and died for was the right of trial by jury. This was my heritage, stained sacred by their blood, and it devolved upon me to stand up for it. All right, I threatened to myself; just wait till he gets to me.

He got to me. My name… was called, and I stood up. The bailiff said, "Vagrancy, your Honor," and I began to talk. But the judge began talking at the same time, and he said, "Thirty days." I started to protest, but at that moment his Honor was calling the name of the next hobo on the list. His Honor paused long enough to say to me, "Shut up!" The bailiff forced me to sit down. And the next moment that next hobo had received thirty days and the succeeding hobo was just in process of getting his.

…I was dazed. Here was I, under sentence, after a farce of a trial wherein I was denied not only my right of trial by jury, but my right to plead guilty or not guilty.…But when I asked for a lawyer, I was laughed at.

Jack London and the other hobos were all handcuffed in pairs and marched down the streets of Niagara Falls to the train station, watched by tourists and passersby. They were taken to the Erie County Penitentiary. In The Road *he writes at length about his experiences in prison.*

Hobo Chieftains Voice
Resentment of Vagrancy Law

"It's 'Guilty, Sixty Days,' With No Recourse for Us," Says Kruse.

CONVENTION OPENS TODAY
"Millionaire Bo" Advocates Industrial and International Peace.

The toad beneath the harrow knows
Exactly where each toothpoint goes;
The butterfly beside the road
Preaches contentment to that toad.
— Kipling

From *Buffalo Courier*, January 30, 1917. p. 4.

Generally speaking, that expresses the attitude of the hoboes of the United States toward society. The delegates to the national convention of the Migratory Workers of the World which opens at No. 259 Main street at 10 o'clock this morning say that they and those they represent are thoroughly familiar with harrows and as thoroughly tired of preaching. They are not contented, they want to better their condition by attracting the attention of the public to their grievances and so they are holding this national convention.

The delegates may not be fashion plates, but they are far from being ragged vagabonds, yet each one of them has been arrested anywhere from once to a score of times for vagrancy. They are defraying their own expenses, although those for railroad fare are not heavy, and they are tremendously in earnest.

Plan No Spectacular Stunts.

"We are not here to pull off any spectacular stunts," said National Secretary John X. Kelly, yesterday, "but we are trying to better the condition of the migratory worker, or hobo as the public calls him. We want better working conditions and freedom from the unjust and tyrannical vagrancy laws. Every man's hand is against us except when they want us in a case of dire necessity such as harvest time or in the fruit picking season. Aside from such occasions it is the jail or the rock pile for us. We are serious and thoughtful men. We realize that we are an indispensible factor in the great industrial progress of the nation, and we are tired of being treated worse than slaves."

Dr. James Eads How, the "millionaire hobo," wealthy but as democratic as the poorest of his brethren, prone to soft shirts and shabby attire, is one of the leaders. Dr. How is an idealist and an enthusiast. He quotes freely from the Scriptures.

"I sincerely hope," he said yesterday, "that we will be able to arrange a public joint debate between Dr. Irvin St. John Tucker, president of the Hobo college of Chicago, and the Rev William A. Sunday. I should like to invite rabbis, Catholic priests and clergy of every denomination to hear the two men discuss the question of peace. There was a message to the brotherhood of man, to all migratory workers, that was given in Galilee some centuries ago, but in all I have read of Mr. Sunday's utterances he has never alluded to it. That message is full of international peace—universal peace—and I should like to hear Mr. Sunday attempt to controvert Mr. Tuckers views on the question.

Suggest Hobo Breakfast.

"My idea is to have a regular 'hobo breakfast,' which necessarily will be inexpensive, some morning before the convention closes to which the clergy and the public would be invited, and to follow with the debate. We shall make the offer to Mr. Sunday and I hope he accepts.

"Peace is our central idea in this movement. We want industrial peace and international peace. I believe that this horrible war will be settled by the workingmen who are now fighting in the trenches. If it is settled in any other way there will be revolutions that may be more terrible than war itself."

National President Charles Kruse is leading the campaign for the repeal of vagrancy laws.

"After we are through work on the big jobs," he said yesterday, "we cease to become units of society. When we leave the harvest fields of the west, the fruit belts of the middle west or east or the construction camps of the south we are picked up as vagrants in the first town we come to, no matter whether we have money or not, fined so heavily that it leaves us penniless, and in addition sent to prison or workhouse, so that officials may grow rich and fat on the fees they get for arresting and convicting us."

No Recourse, He Says

"We are not allowed to plead or say anything in our defense once we are in court. 'Guilty: sixty days,' is the usual formula, and we have no recourse. In the south it is even worse. In some states a man who is working out his fine in prison at the rate of ten cents a day is often auctioned off to a contractor who pays the city or county as high as seventy-five cents a day for his services. I spent thirty days in a hell like that in Mississippi and I have never recovered from the physical effects of it.

"But lawyers are beginning to realize the injustice of the vagrancy laws, and many have told me that they are clearly unconstitutional. We are going to keep on working until that great wrong is redressed."

More delegates arrived yesterday and an attendance of nearly 100 is expected when the convention is called to order. The first day will be devoted to routine business largely, but there is no telling what some impetuous "Bo" will set off.

Fierce Fight with Hobo on President's Train

Secret Service Man Grabs Tramp by the Leg and the Fellow Puts Up a Vigorous Resistance—Glass Is Smashed and There Is Much Excitement

From the *Milwaukee Journal*, Apr. 25, 1903, p. 1.

Gillette, Wyo., Apr 25—The secret service men on the president's train had an exciting mix-up with a tramp last night. A man was seen between the baggage and club cars on the outside of the vestibule. One of the officers raised a window and started to grab the man, when the latter aimed a blow at him through the glass, shattering it.

The officer caught the man's leg and succeeded in getting him into the car, where he showed fight. He was a powerful man and it took some time before he was overpowered and handcuffed.

A card found on him shows his identification as Edward Russell, a sailor member of the Sailors' union of San Francisco. When the train reached Billings he was turned over to the police. When asked why he was on the train, Russell said he wanted to reach St. Paul, where his mother lived.

A second report confirms the presence and arrest of a hobo on the presidential train.

Tramp Found on the Train

A Hobo Rode Through Montana on President's Special

From *The Pittsburgh Press*, Apr. 26, 1903, p. 23.

Gillette, Wyo., Apr 25—The President's special made a night run through Montana and entered Wyoming without especial incident, save the discovery of a tramp soon after leaving Evanston. The train was running at a high rate of speed when one of the secret service men discovered the man on the vestibule between the baggage and buffet cars. As soon as the tramp saw the detective he struck at him through the glass, smashing the pane. The detective then grabbed the tramp's foot as the latter was ascending to the top of the car and dragged him down.

When he was finally landed safely inside the car he was handcuffed and placed inside the baggage car. He gave his name as E. Russell. He showed a member's card in the seamen's union of San Francisco and said he was on his way to St. Paul. He said he did not know he was on the President's train but was glad of it. The authorities at Billings took charge of him.

The Hobo Was Nabbed

Had the Nerve to Invade President Taft's Special Car, Mayflower

From the *Troy Northern Budget*, Nov. 14, 1909, p. 1.

Washington, Nov. 13—A hobo seeking shelter from a ticket hunter conductor on the Federal express from Boston to Washington, wandered hapless into President Taft's car, the Mayflower, locked himself into the kitchen and created the greatest excitement of all the President's travels.

"Jimmie" Sloan of the secret service was given the rare opportunity of distinguishing himself by making a real arrest, while Will Anderson and Ed Letcher, the two presidential porters of the Pullman service, became real heroes.

The incident occurred just outside of Bridgeport, Conn., and it was to the authorities of that town that the hobo was delivered by the intrepid Sloan. President Taft's car was switched on to the Federal express at New Haven shortly after midnight. Two local day coaches had been placed on the express ahead of the President's car and it was from one of these that the hobo found the way into the Mayflower.

Letcher, when he discovered the tramp crouched in the corner of the kitchen almost turned white, but in another minute he had pounced on the wanderer. "Letch" called for Anderson and Anderson called for "Jimmie" Sloan.

"Jimmie" said a few polite things to the tramp, who claimed at first to be a brakeman on the New Haven road. He was immediately disowned by the train crew and at Bridgeport was handed over to the police. The President meanwhile was snoozing away in the stateroom at the rear end of the car in blissful ignorance of the excitement.

HOBOS AS HEROES

Not all hobos were unwelcome, however. Some were recognized as heroes, finding that their knowledge, talents, quick thinking, and powers of observation were highly appreciated and rewarded by others.

Where Tramps Are Welcome

Interesting Story Surrounds a Stately Mansion in Ohio

From *The Reading Eagle*, Reading, PA, October 12, 1902, p. 12.

Geneva, Ohio: There is an imposing mansion in this village, where tramps are never turned away. It was built by the late George W. Hopper.

Years ago Hopper was a poor young man. He received but little schooling, and his education was very limited. In early youth he became identified with the Standard Oil Company, being given the management of the department where barrels were painted before they were filled with oil. Though the barrels were thoroughly painted on the outside, the oil would soak through them, and in a short time the paint would peel off and allow the oil to seep out. The company was considerably hampered in this way, and many were the experiments tried to alleviate the difficulty, but without success.

One day, while Hopper was pondering over the question, a tramp walked up, and hearing Hopper lament that the barrels could not be painted so they would hold oil, he said: "I'll tell you how to fix them. Fill them with water and then paint them. When they are dry pour out the water, and the water in the wood will stay in and prevent the oil from soaking through and cutting the paint."

Rather dubious of the success of the tramp's suggestion, Hopper tried it, and the scheme worked successfully. The advancement and royalties Hopper received from this idea soon resulted in wealth, and when he died a few years ago, his fortune was estimated at from $2,000,000 to $3,500,000.

Hopper's stepping stone to wealth has long ago been succeeded by better ways of making barrels unleakable, but the idea given Hopper by the tramp was the means of securing for him the vast fortune he possessed. After retiring from active business life Hopper offered to make the tramp rich, and although a reward of $25,000 was offered for the tramp's appearance, none ever came to claim the money nor has anything ever been heard of the tramp.

Out of gratitude to this one tramp, the whole army of tramps receive a benefit, for no matter how disreputable or seedy looking a tramp may be, he is always given a square meal at the Hopper home, even on to this day. Charles Hopper now occupies the home built by his father nearly a dozen years ago.

This story was included, in abbreviated form, in a tour of architecture included in a book of Ohio history compiled by WPA workers in 1940.

—from *The Ohio Guide*, compiled by Workers of the Writer's Program of the Works Progress Administration in the State of Ohio. Oct. 1940.

GENEVA, 26.5 m. (685 alt., 4,166 pop.)…At 30 m. is the junction with a country road.

Left on this road is the HOPPER MANSION (R.) , 0.8 m., a sprawling house of lonely mien. Near the end of the nineteenth century—so the story goes—a hobo cadged a meal from George Hopper, a Standard Oil employee. Hopper mentioned to him the ticklish problem of preventing oil from permeating the wooden barrels used as containers; the hobo casually suggested a solution and resumed his journey. The stranger's formula worked. When Hopper, a grateful man, built this mansion for himself, he ordered that it be always open to 'men of the road.'

"Hobo Joe" Poet Sings of Millerton

Fair Town Never Had a Poet Before, but Now—
Editor Appreciates His Verse

Modestly He Proclaims His Poverty of Fame,
but He Breathes the Air of Kings

Special to *The New York Times*
From *The New York Times*, July 31, 1904.

POUGHKEEPSIE, July 30—A cheerful-looking individual, with rubicund visage, keen blue eyes, and garments the worse for wear, strolled into the village of Millerton, the fairest of all Dutchess County, yesterday. Until his arrival all Millerton had labored under a heavy cloud of sadness. To-day all Millerton is bursting with pride and joy. Before "Hobo Joe" Thornton's ragged trousers had come to town, Millerton mourned the lack of a poet to emulate the lofty verse of the bards of Rhinebeck, "Beautiful, Republican Rhinebeck," Pawling, and Dover. With "Hobo Joe's" arrival all has changed, the darkness has been dissipated, the sadness is gone.

On "Hobo Joe's" arrival here he went straight to the office of Col. Card, the village editor. With little formality and less embarrassment he proceeded to lay before the editorial mind the exigencies of a life on the road.

He began by observing cheerfully that Millerton appeared to be a right thrifty sort of place, and followed this with informations that he and thriftiness had long been strangers.

Editor Card is a philosopher and a philanthropist. A few minutes later the tramp was savagely enjoying a hearty meal. Between bites he allowed that in the vicissitudes of life he had been worse treated. There was a certain Mrs. Cole he held in scorn, who had given him two dry, thin slices of bread for a repast. He hummed meditatively:

My dear Mrs. Cole,
Your heart and your soul
Were revealed in those slices of bread.

"Indeed, you are a poet!" exclaimed the amazed editor.
"I am, most excellent Sir," proudly replied "Hobo Joe."
No trumpet of fame is sounding my name,
No silver or gold have I got;
Not title I claim of ancestors' shame,
No mansion, no castle, no cot.
But I breathe the air of Princes and Kings,
Gaze on the same sky above,
Knowing the Master ordered all things
With wisdom and fitness and love.

"Hobo Joe" also showed an unusual willingness to work for the occasional dimes and hand-outs that came his way. It was in this way that Millerton came to be enshrined in the niche of fame by "Hobo Joe." Under the inspiration of Editor Card's bounteous favor the poetic muse evolved this tribute:

Fair Millerton on the Harlem Road,
I'd gladly choose as an abode.
Its paper, breezy, bright, and true,
With news accurate, terse, and new,
Tells what's going on at home, afar,
And all about the Japan war.
Fair Millerton, Fair Millerton, in truth, it's best indeed thou art.
And I am loath, Fair Millerton, in truth, from thee to part.

Before saying farewell to Millerton's freehanded hospitality "Hobo Joe" paid his respects to "Field Marshal" Lou Payn's constituents in Chatham, who had used him despitefully and cast him out, as follows:

When God created man, we're told,
He formed them out of dust;
While some of them retained their mold,
Some others of them bust.
He looked them o'er, picked out the whole,
And made them perfect men,
The others were not worth a soul,
To Chatham he sent them,
And so it is that Chatham's race
Are never classed with men;
No soul, no heart—but in their place
The gizzard of a hen.

Reads Just Like a Thrilling Chapter in a Work of Fiction

Humble Hobo, Counting the Ties, Finds a Split Rail On the Central Near Walworth Station, Flags Express Train, Saves the Passengers, Received Purse of $22, Has More Honors in Store

From *Rochester Democrat and Chronicle*, Sept. 1, 1904, p.3.

Aug. 31—The idea that the much-caricatured and persecuted tramp has no place on this celestial sphere and that the "hobo" nuisance should be banished from the country received a severe shock here late last night. The story of two prominent citizens of this place, who happened to be on the Boston express, the east-bound train, No. 42, which passed this station at 7:48 in the evening, that a tramp had held up the train and saved them from a wreck, changed the impression of the "dusty knight of the road" from disgust to admiration.

The hero's name is Fred Bibby and gave his address as nowhere in particular. He was "counting the ties" along the Central, going from Buffalo to New York, and when nearing Walworth station he discovered a rail had been split on track one and was out of place. With all possible speed he ran to the station and informed the agent, Michael Haley, who was skeptical at first, but on being urged went back with the tramp to the spot where the break was. They were just in time, as they could see the express train coming in the distance. They commenced to yell and wave the lantern. The engineer saw them and the train came to a stop within a short distance of the break.

The exertion had been too much for "Weary Willie," and he fainted away. He was picked up, taken on the cars and revived. The train backed to a switch and came down on another track, an hour late. Bibby was taken through to Syracuse. In the meantime he was lionized by the passengers, who passed a hat for him and obtained a collection of $22.

He accepted the gift and said he was a mechanic and looking for work. He was walking along the track and almost stumbled over a broken piece of rail, which lay about four feet from the gap in the rail. His mechanical instincts caused him to measure the broken piece with a rule he always carried, and found it to be just twelve inches long.

The Central officials will probably make some recognition of the prompt work of Bibby, as had the train pounded over the gap, derailment would undoubtedly have followed.

Hobo Saves Girls' Lives, Is Rewarded

Riding a Boxcar to Dying Mother, He Saw Fire and Gave Alarm

(Special Telegram to Gazette Times)

from the *Pittsburgh Post Gazette*, April 6, 1912, p. 3

Chicago, Ill., Apr. 6—Joseph Foley of New York, whom ill luck had made a tramp, saw flames burst through the roof of a building in Oak Park today as he was riding by in a box car. He jumped off in time to give an alarm, probably saving the lives of 20 girls. For his reward he received a railroad ticket to St. Louis, where his mother is dying, and enough money to help him when he arrives in that city.

Incidentally—and this is no small matter to Foley—he discovered after the fire was out that the train he thought was carrying him home was really carrying him to Omaha, and he would have been carried 500 miles out of his way.

The building was that of the Morton Millinery Company and the girls employed there were unaware of their danger. Fire starting from sparks blown from a bonfire from a neighboring yard was spreading over the roof and upper stories of the building. Foley saw it, jumped off a train, ran to the building and shouted a warning. Then he sought a telephone. Later he helped the girls from the burning building.

An insurance adjuster reached the building as the firemen were leaving. Foley was pointed out as the man who gave the alarm.

"Well, that fellow deserves the best we've got," said the adjuster. "He's saved the lives of these girls. Take me to him."

Foley told his story. When he came to the part about his mother, the insurance man went down into his pocket and produced a roll of bills and handed several to the hobo.

"Now," he said, "come along with me and I'll see that you ride to St. Louis on velvet and eat your meals in the dining car."

Later Foley rode out of Chicago with a lower berth, and the dining car conductor had orders to give him everything from soup to nuts.

Tramp Rides on Velvet

Wins Parlor Car Journey by Giving Timely Fire Alarm

(Special to *The New York Times*)

published April 6, 1912

Chicago, April 5—Joseph Foley of New York, whom ill-luck had made a tramp, saw flames burst through the roof of a building in Oak Park to-day as he was riding by in a box car. He jumped off the train in time to give an alarm that probably saved the lives of a number of girls. For his reward, he received a railroad ticket to St. Louis, where his mother is dying, and enough money to help him when arrives in that city.

Incidentally, Foley discovered after the fire was out that the train he thought was carrying him South was really carrying him to Omaha. If he had not jumped off the train to give the fire alarm he would have been taken 500 miles out of his way. The building was that of the Morton & Morton Millinery Company, and the girls employed there were unaware of their danger.

An insurance adjuster reached the building as the firemen were leaving, and Foley was pointed out as the man who had given the alarm.

Foley told his story, and when he came to the part about his mother, the insurance man went down into his pocket and produced a roll of bills. He slipped off a few and handed them to the hobo.

"Now," he said, "come along with me and I'll see that you ride to St. Louis on velvet and eat your meals in the dining car."

Sergt. Eagan Finds His Hobo Guest

Police Officer Once More Fulfills His
Christmas Task of Feasting Wanderer

From *The Gazette Times*, Pittsburgh, Dec. 26, 1912, p. 11.

The happiest man in Pittsburgh today is James W. Eagan, sergeant at the Mt. Washington Police Station. The peace that passeth knowledge is his. And some place there is a hobo in whose mind still lingers the visions of a steaming turkey, ambrosia of smoking plum pudding and the consciousness of palate gratified.

It all came as a surprise to the hobo—this invitation to a big dinner with a police sergeant—but with Mr. Eagan it was all planned. He knew he was going to have a hobo at his table yesterday, but who the lucky one would be he didn't know until Christmas eve, when a weary stranger showed up in the police station and applied for a night's lodging. It is an old story, but the sergeant repeats it to his tramp Christmas guest every year.

Some 3 years ago Sergt. Eagan was doing a little Christmas tramping himself, in New Orleans, La., and while he was passing a rich home he spied a fat turkey steaming on a plate. An application for a "handout" was refused him, and since that time the sergeant has made it a point to feed some wanderer on each Christmas. Sergt. Eagan insists that his guest must be a real hobo, and he declared that yesterday's friend amply filled requirements.

In the late 1800s, a group of hobos got together to form a union for the purpose of avoiding prosecution for vagrancy while they traveled looking for work. A person who was a union member would not be prosecuted for being unemployed. Because the founding members numbered 63, they called themselves Tourist Union No. 63.

TOURIST UNION #63

An ethical code was created by Tourist Union #63 during its 1889 National Hobo Convention in St. Louis, Missouri. This code was voted upon as a concrete set of laws to govern the Nationwide Hobo Body; it reads this way:

1. Decide your own life, don't let another person run or rule you.
2. When in town, always respect the local law and officials, and try to be a gentleman at all times.
3. Don't take advantage of someone who is in a vulnerable situation, locals or other hobos.
4. Always try to find work, even if temporary, and always seek out jobs nobody wants. By doing so you not only help a business along, but ensure employment should you return to that town again.
5. When no employment is available, make your own work by using your added talents at crafts.
6. Do not allow yourself to become a stupid drunk and set a bad example for locals' treatment of other hobos.
7. When jungling in town, respect handouts, do not wear them out, another hobo will be coming along who will need them as bad, if not worse than you.
8. Always respect nature, do not leave garbage where you are jungling.
9. If in a community jungle, always pitch in and help.
10. Try to stay clean, and boil up wherever possible.

11. When traveling, ride your train respectfully, take no personal chances, cause no problems with the operating crew or host railroad, act like an extra crew member.

12. Do not cause problems in a train yard, another hobo will be coming along who will need passage through that yard.

13. Do not allow other hobos to molest children, expose all molesters to authorities, they are the worst garbage to infest any society.

14. Help all runaway children, and try to induce them to return home.

15. Help your fellow hobos whenever and wherever needed, you may need their help someday.

16. If present at a hobo court and you have testimony, give it. Whether for or against the accused, your voice counts!

Tuck, a hobo and member of Tourist Union #63,
sits outside the Hobo Museum in Britt, Iowa.

KEEPERS OF HOBO HISTORY

The Hobo Foundation and Museum

The following information is from the Hobo Museum's website. Reprinted by permission.

The separate dreams of three hobos came together in 1974 when they realized they shared the common goal of preserving hobo history. Hood River Blackie's search for steam-era hobos brought him to Britt and introduced him to Steamtrain Maury and Feather River John. They drew up their letter of incorporation, filed for tax-exempt status, and along with several Britt locals, became the Hobo Foundation.

Today, the Foundation carries on the ambitious goals of these original hobos.

The Hobo Foundation owns and operates the Hobo Museum in Britt, Iowa, and maintains the Hobo Cemetery in East Britt.

Since 1980, the Hobo Foundation has been operating the Hobo Museum in a building that was formerly the Chief Theater. Located at 51 Main Avenue South, Britt, Iowa, 50423, the Hobo Museum is a popular tourist attraction, especially during the National Hobo Convention held each August.

The Hobo Museum currently contains extensive memorabilia of such famous hobos as Steamtrain Maury, Frisco Jack, Connecticut Slim, Slo Motion Shorty, Hard Rock Kid, and Pennsylvania Kid, just to name a few, plus original hobo crafts, photographs, videos and documentaries depicting the hobo lifestyle, paintings, a historic postcard collection, a hobo doll collection and much more. The Hobo Museum is a tribute to all the hobos who helped build America into the great country it is today.

PART II—HOBO TRADITIONS

The National Hobo Convention has been held annually in Britt, Iowa, since 1900, when officials in Britt invited Tourist Union #63 to move their convention to Britt. The hobos accepted the invitation, and the convention continues to be held on the second weekend in August. The hobo jungle and all the activities are open to the public; visitors are welcome to take photographs, talk with the hobos, learn some of the hobo traditions, and enjoy the entertainment. In this section, I describe the events and share my thoughts and observations as I attended the 2011 convention.

For a schedule of events, check out the website at
http://www.brittiowa.com/hobo/events.htm.

The hobo section of the Evergreen Cemetery in Britt.

When my life on earth is done
Let me ride the Westbound to the land beyond the sun
If it's all the same to you, there's one thing that I want to do
Let me ride to heaven on a train

—From "Let Me Ride to Heaven on a Train"
By Liberty Justice

HONORING THOSE WHO HAVE CAUGHT THE WESTBOUND

At the northeast corner of the Evergreen Cemetery in Britt stands a tall, sturdy cross constructed of railroad ties. Next to it is a section of a split-rail fence, and close to that is a narrow concrete column about four feet tall and perhaps four inches square. A red bandana is tied to the top of the column, and just below the point of the bandana the words "Unknown Hobo" are carved into one side. In front of and behind the cross, perpendicular to the road, are two neat rows of grave markers. A few are granite and have been professionally carved, but most are made of thick concrete, set flush with the ground, and have been hand carved by a fellow hobo.

That day, a small red wagon bearing a handmade concrete grave marker, still in its wooden mold, had been pulled onto the grass. The ground in front of the wagon was freshly dug—grass and dirt had been scraped away in the shape of a rectangle sized to receive the marker. The small silver-colored spade that had made the excavation lay under the wagon. In the center of the rectangle was a deeper, round hole that had been hollowed out to accept an entire coffee can, which would hold the cremated remains of the man who had "caught the Westbound"—hobo parlance for a traveler who had died.

We were attending the first of two hobo memorial ceremonies that would be performed in the cemetery. There would be another later in the week that was open to the public, but this ceremony was private, and we had been invited by Minnesota Jewel and Tuck—two hobos we met on our first evening in Britt. Hobos were slowly arriving, many ambling across the cemetery with walking sticks. People who hadn't seen each other in a while hugged each other. A grizzled old-timer with a tan bucket hat and full white beard started tuning up his banjo.

I watched as two hobos lifted the concrete marker from the little red wagon and lowered it for a practice placement on the grave. Satisfied with its fit, they set the marker back on the wagon.

The service didn't appear close to starting yet, so I walked toward the wagon to get a better look. On the marker, which I learned Tuck had made, *Road Hog USA, Hobo King* had been carved into the concrete when it was still wet. For the ceremony, several pictures had been placed on top, temporarily obscuring Road Hog's time span on this earth. A striped railroad cap sat in the middle of the marker, with a large owl or hawk feather wedged into it.

I walked further, following the line of markers positioned in the cemetery grass. Each marker was adorned with a small American flag attached to a wooden stick that was either pushed into the ground next to the grave or, if the hobo was a veteran, inserted into the metal service flag holder. At the base of each stick, a red bandana had been carefully rolled into a circular shape, as if it was ready to be worn around a hobo's neck. As I passed one marker after the other, I noticed the care that had been taken to make them and personalize them.

Some hobos were buried alone:

Fry Pan Jack
Hobo King
1912 – 1990

Where the dash would normally separate his dates, a small cast iron fry pan
had been embedded into the concrete.

On some markers, instead of a dash, a railroad spike was embedded:

Joseph D. Baker
Hobo Joe
Feb 13 1931 – Sept 18 2000

Cinder Box Cindy
Hobo Queen
Jan 26, 53 – Jan 21, 02

Some hobos are buried with their spouses:

The Whittler
Adolph and Adeline Vandertie

No dates were given for this couple, but a pocketknife and railroad spike
were embedded in their marker.

Many of the hobos were veterans, and some of them have a granite
marker provided by the government:

Jerome L. Justice
A3C US Air Force
Korea
Jul 12 1935 – Apr 23 2008
National Hobo Troubadour
Liberty Justice

Liberty dollar coins had been attached to his gravestone. Later, I would hear his music, which was played often at the convention—at the ladies' tea, around the campfire, and so on.

A few hobos had done some funeral preplanning. "Here's where I'm going to be," Redbird Express said, pointing to his marker. His was one of the larger granite markers, professionally engraved. It read:

"Redbird Express"
Karl E. Teller
Hobo King 2002–2003

A Union Pacific steam locomotive, tender, and boxcar stretches across the stone, with the caption *Big Boy Steam Locomotive* underneath it, in script. Centered under the locomotive are these words: He Did Things His Way, "Most of the Time". On the left, his birth date—July 15, 1941—has already been carved. Opposite his birth date the granite is blank, waiting for completion, for the date he catches the westbound. The Union Pacific logo and one final statement were carved into the very bottom edge: Redbird Is Riding the West Bound.

As more hobos arrived, they were offered small bags of ashes if they wanted them. This is part of the hobo tradition. These were Road Hog USA's ashes. The hobos, in the spirit of their close-knit community, had taken up a collection when they heard of Road Hog's death, and sent another hobo, Frog, to get the ashes so he could be buried in Britt. Only some of Road Hog USA's ashes would be buried in the coffee can under his marker, though. Many of those who took ashes would take them on their trips and fling the ashes from the road or from a train so that their hobo friend would always be free and traveling. Some take ashes to their home campfires and other hobo gatherings, and then bring back ashes from those campfires to the next year's hobo convention—creating a connection and symmetry.

Road Hog loved and collected feathers, and the hobos passed out feathers from his collection to anyone who wanted one. By the time the service began, there were feathers everywhere—sticking out of people's hats, hair, shirt pockets, and overalls.

Connecticut Shorty, who had been his Hobo Queen in 1992, read her tribute to Road Hog, which brought tears to my eyes even though I never knew him. Then, anyone who wanted to could share a memory and/or place an object with some meaning to be buried in the grave. Some hobos added a feather. Another remembered a favorite belt buckle, which, as it was discovered, Road Hog had given to one hobo, who had given it to another hobo, and so on, until it found its way back to its original owner that day at the cemetery. Tuck, although not yet aware of the buckle's history, had embedded it into Road Hog's marker. *Full circle*, I thought.

After all who wished to speak had their say, Luther the Jet, in his clear voice, sang "Big Rock Candy Mountain"—a traditional hobo song made famous by such people as Burl Ives (himself a hobo), Roger Whittaker, and more recently, in the movie *O Brother Where Art Thou*. The song describes a hobo's idea of paradise, and it made people smile a little, easing their sadness. There are many variations on the lyrics, but Luther sang it this way, *a capella*:

One evening as the sun went down
And the jungle fire was burning
Down the path came a hobo hiking
And he said, Boys, I'm not turning
I'm going to a land that's far away
Beside the crystal fountain
So come along with me, we're going to see
The Big Rock Candy Mountain

In the Big Rock Candy Mountain
There's a land so fair and bright
Where the boxcars all are empty
And you sleep out every night
Where the handouts grow on bushes
And the sun shines every day
On the birds and the bees

And the cigarette trees
And the lemonade springs
Where the bluebird sings
On the Big Rock Candy Mountain

In the Big Rock Candy Mountain
The cops have wooden legs
And the bulldogs all have rubber teeth
And the hens lay soft-boiled eggs
The farmers' trees are full of fruit
And the barns are full of hay
And I'm bound to go
Where there ain't no snow
Where the rain don't fall
And the wind don't blow
In the Big Rock Candy Mountain

In the Big Rock Candy Mountain
You never change your socks
And the little streams of alcohol
Come a tricklin' down the rocks
There ain't no short-handled shovels
No axes, picks, or spades
And I'm bound to stay
Where they sleep all day
Where they hung the jerk
That invented work
In the Big Rock Candy Mountain

In the Big Rock Candy Mountain
The jails are made of tin
And you can walk right out again
Just as soon as you go in

There the railroad bulls have all gone blind
And the shacks all tip their hats
There's a lake of stew
And a gin lake too
You can paddle all around 'em
In a big canoe
In the Big Rock Candy Mountain

The crowd applauded appreciatively for Luther, and the ceremony ended informally. Many of the hobos stayed to talk, and remember. Tomorrow they would return for the public ceremony.

THE PUBLIC HOBO MEMORIAL SERVICE

The Hobo Memorial Service was listed on the convention schedule for Friday at 9 a.m. As we arrived at the cemetery, it was immediately obvious that this was a different kind of event from what we had witnessed yesterday. The narrow lanes that wound through the graveyard were lined with cars, as was the main road that passed outside the cemetery near the hobo section. A large crowd gathered; hobos were joined by townspeople and convention-goers.

A military honor guard detail had assembled. Four stood near what would be the grave of Iowa Blackie, a Vietnam vet. Three of the guard held flags: a Veterans of Foreign War flag, an Iowa veterans flag, and an American flag. The fourth man stood at attention, his right hand raised in salute. At a signal, they joined four other members of the honor guard. Seven vets pointed their guns into the air and fired the traditional three-volley salute. The eighth man stood apart and held a bugle to his lips as a recording played "Taps."

The hobo named Black Knight stepped up to a microphone to start the remembrances. Three hobos had caught the westbound this past year: Road Hog USA, who was memorialized yesterday, Iowa Blackie, well-known to the community as a hobo poet, and Railroad Randy, who was killed by a drunk driver while he was riding his bike to attend this convention. Black Knight started with Iowa Blackie:

"What can you say about Iowa Blackie? Those of you that knew him knew he was a cantankerous old character at times, he was lovable at times, and at all times he was a great poet. But if you tried to read the writing you couldn't do it. If you took a magnifying glass, it was almost like it was typewritten. The man had a lot of talents. He sold his books for anything over a dollar—even a dollar and a penny he would accept," Black Knight grinned. "I believe all of us need an Iowa Blackie in our lives to make it complete. So at this time, I'd like all of us to think, 'Iowa Blackie, I hope you have a wonderful eternity.'"

Black Knight stepped away from the mic and another hobo came up to speak: "He [Iowa Blackie] and I started coming to Britt together and he had a fierce pride in his hobo culture because he learned an awful lot about it before he entered it. I want to read one of the first poems he wrote:

Since I was fourteen years of age
A hobo life would be my goal
Not caring for a living wage
Preferring on the rails to roll.

If any teachers had then known
What my ambition was to be
They might have little patience shown
Since few of them had ever been so free.

"He had so much pride… he could outthink and outsmart his teachers. They had no idea the lifestyle he was going to lead."

He stepped away and Black Knight returned to introduce Minneapolis Jewel, who would share her thoughts on Railroad Randy.

"I was a very lucky person one day in south Minneapolis," Jewel began in her assured, commanding voice. She was affable and energetic as she told a story, capturing the attention of her hobo friends and hardly pausing to take a breath. "I was coming out of this store that sells herbs, etcetera, and here was a funny looking guy with a funny looking hat standing by my truck, looking, because my truck has license plates 'MS HOBO' on it. So I got to talking and I happened to have some hobo guides, and I told him, 'You've got to come down to Britt. We'd love to have you.' And he said, 'Yes, I will.' So he showed up down here.

"Everybody that knows Randy knows that his smile was so infectious… his joy of being with people. And the thing I have to laugh at is that he was such a flirt with women. He didn't care how old you were. We had a party last year—our King and Queen party—and Randy came, and my mom came up from Wisconsin, and she asked, 'Who's that guy that wears that

hat?' And I said, 'Yeah I know, he looks like Gabby Hayes.' And she said, 'Well, I don't know…he's kind of hitting on me or something.'" The crowd laughed and nodded, and Jewel laughed, too. "Yeah, my mom!" Jewel said, "And she got a kick out of it."

"Everybody who talked to him enjoyed him so much," Jewel continued. "In March, he called. He was so proud—he got a display case at the Walker Library in the uptown area. It was a glass case in the lobby, and me and Angie Dirty Feet went over to see it. He must have had 50 photographs, and under each photograph was a caption of what, who, and whatever. To him, this was his family. He just loved it that he was in the library. And at the end of the month, the person who was supposed to have the display case didn't show up, so they extended his show for another month.

"We love him," Jewel concluded. "That's all I can say. He gave us a lot of memories in a short time, and he was a good guy all the way."

A stocky man with dark brown hair extending to the middle of his back was next to speak. He wore a charcoal jacket, black pants, a printed vest topped by a white pleated shirt, and a black bowtie. He was introduced as Marty Gage, brother of Iowa Blackie.

"A lot of people here probably knew him better than me, but I guess I did try to emulate him. Many years ago I took a trip on the rails to Hampton in late December. I really didn't think much about the cold when I got started, but I sure did by time I was done. The trouble was, the train didn't stop in Hampton. So I made a jump for it and I hit so hard. One of my snow boots came off—I never did find that damn thing, even next spring. Fortunately, I lived within a couple of blocks from the tracks so I was able to get there and warm up.

"I was also very fortunate, even though a lot of people did know him better than me in the last 10 or 15 years, I did happen to see him for the first time in over a decade this past summer. That was very gratifying to me and I feel pretty good about that. I also feel good about the fact that I was able to acquire his Harley, which I know was his dream bike, and frankly it was also mine for the longest time." The crowd laughed, and so did Marty, adding, "And I told him I was officially jealous!" He paused. "That's about all I have to share."

I thought about the complicated story that Marty had distilled into a couple minutes for this occasion and how there was probably a lot of unspoken pain in his and Iowa Blackie's life stories. But Marty came for his brother's memorial service, and it seemed right that he had a chance to speak.

Other friends and supporters who had caught the westbound the past year were acknowledged next: Wanda Graham, wife of Steam Train Maury; Hippie Hobo, another friend of Steam Train's from Toledo; and Anna, a friend of FLC and who was recognized for being very helpful around the jungle for many years.

The Roll Call

Two hobos, Inkman and Indiana Hobo II, prepared to give the roll call, the part of the ceremony in which departed hobos are remembered by name.

Inkman began: "Now comes the time for us to remember our family that has caught the westbound. These are not just names but actual people who have gone before us to make a better life for us when we catch up with them. They may not all be from military service, but they were in a greater service nonetheless—the service for betterment of life for their fellow man."

Briefly, another man took the microphone to direct the next part of the tradition: "While they're reading the roll call of the hobos, let's start our ceremony with the walking sticks. Tap your walking sticks on each of the stones, because as long as we remember them, they're not dead."

Hobos walk slowly beside the graves of those who have caught the Westbound.
They tap their walking sticks on each gravestone in remembrance.

"Hobos buried in Britt," Inkman said: "The Hard Rock Kid, Mountain Dew, Slow Motion Shorty...."

Hobos formed a line and slowly walked the rows of gravestones, gently tapping their walking sticks on each one as Inkman and Indiana Hobo II took turns reading a long list of names:

"Pennsylvania Kid...Iowa Bob...Slim Jim...Calamity Jane... Derail... Fishbones...Liberty Justice...Cinderbox Cindy... Fry Pan Jack..."

I stood back and watched as the hobos paused to reflect, touching their sticks on each grave marker. Their walking sticks were as varied as the hobos themselves. The upper half of one tall stick was carved into a spiral and topped off with a red, white, and blue ribbon and a bronze American eagle. The lower half of another, made of dark wood, had been carved into a deep, gnarly corkscrew. Some were plainer sticks with feathers and bandanas attached to them. Others bore carved patterns and symbols. One woman used her native American flute to tap each grave.

When Inkman and Indiana Hobo II finished reading the names of hobos buried in Britt, they began remembering hobos buried elsewhere: Hippie Hobo…Banjo Fred…Scoop Shovel Scottie. Hood River Blackie… Colorado Ed…The Drifter…Sonny Slim Chance… Boxcar Willie… Thirty-Weight Earl…Horizontal John…Stagger Lee…Woody Guthrie… Jack London… Burl Ives…Harmonica Spike…Sally Lady…Rambling Rudy… Joshua Long Gone…The Unknown Hobo, Minneapolis, Minnesota…Hard Rock Cajun…Gas Can Patty…

Finally, when all the names had been read, the trio of hobo women called Serenity sang a closing hymn:

LIFE'S RAILWAY TO HEAVEN

Life is like a mountain railway
With an engineer that's brave
We must make the run successful
From the cradle to the grave
Watch the curves, the fills, the tunnels
Never falter, never fail
Keep your hands upon the throttle
And your eyes upon the rail

You will often find obstructions
Look for storms and wind and rain
On a fill, or curve, or trestle
They will almost ditch your train
Put your trust alone in Jesus
Never falter, never fail
Keep your hands upon the throttle
And your eyes upon the rail

THE HOBO CAMPFIRE

Imagine life without fire: no warmth, no cooked food, no light in the dark, perhaps even no camaraderie. For hobos especially, fire is essential for all those things. Whether in the hobo jungles of the early 1900s or present-day hobo gatherings, the fire is the deep-seated center of the community.

In the old days and in hobo jungles, cooking would have been done over the fire, too. There would have been large tin cans with simmering mulligan stew, or maybe a fry pan set on hot coals to fry fish or potatoes or whatever was at hand. But at the convention, the hobos cooked near the campfire, rather than over it, using a large, multiburner propane stove that provided its own controlled flame.

In Britt, the campfire burned in the jungle throughout the four days of the hobo convention, and most activities—musical performances, poetry readings, a wedding—took place by its flickering light.

The Campfire Lighting Ceremony

The campfire lighting—the official opening ceremony for the National Hobo Convention—began at 7 p.m. on a hot August evening. It was conducted by Redbird Express, who has attended the Britt conventions for twenty-two consecutive years. Redbird wore a red cap and two shirts—a red t-shirt covered by a sleeveless button-front shirt embellished with patches from his travels. He stood near the fire pit, a simple dirt area enclosed by stones. From it rose a pyre of scrap lumber stacked and laid into a pyramid shape and stuffed with newspaper by a young hobo named Marshmallow Kid.

Redbird thanked the Britt Lumber Co. for the wood, credited Marshmallow Kid for building the fire, and welcomed the mayor. He then turned to the crowd and spoke:

"Hello out there to all you hobos and hobos at heart…We're about to light our official fire. We always light our fire with this ceremony at all our hobo gatherings and this convention. Once the fire is lit, it is kept going until the conclusion of the event."

Meanwhile, Marshmallow Kid, to the amusement of the crowd, was soaking the crumpled newspaper with a steady stream of WD 40. I chuckled to myself, thinking that I was witnessing a bit of "cheating." Would it have earned a sneer or a "thumbs up" from old hobos, I wondered.

Redbird directed the Marshmallow Kid to begin lighting the fire— "with a little help from WD40," Redbird joked.

"Is that what they're calling him now?" another hobo laughed.

Marshmallow Kid approached the pit with a lit railroad flare, also called a fusee, and touched it to the paper. As the fire caught and crackled, Redbird began the ceremony, reading from a paper: "There have been all types of fires recorded down through history. Some of these fires include raging fires, hellfires, electrical fires, war fires, and friendly fires. This right here is a friendly fire. So come gather around and witness this event. As the smoke from our fire gets in your clothes, and the light from our fire shines upon your faces, you become one of us—you become part of our hobo circle…

"This fire is the friendliest fire in this country today. We salute the four prevailing winds as we start our fire here. We respect the winds."

Salute to the Four Winds

Redbird motioned for four hobos—Adman, Double B, Dante, and Connecticut Tootsie— to come to the fire. They stepped forward, each carrying a walking stick, and spaced themselves at four points around the fire, turning their backs to the fire.

"First we will salute the north wind," Redbird read. Connecticut Tootsie stood on the north side of the fire; she took the fusee and held it in her outstretched arm, pointing it to the north. All the other hobos raised their sticks and pointed them in the northerly direction.

"The north wind is an ill wind," Redbird continued. "It is a wind of change. It is cool and refreshing. It restores the energy to the earth…and all the crops are harvested. We now salute the north wind."

"Salute," he said. All the hobos answered, saying "salute," in unison.

"Second, we go to the south wind," Redbird said. Connecticut Tootsie handed the fusee to Dante, who pointed it to the south. The hobos picked up their sticks and raised them to the south.

"An old saying goes like this: 'When the wind is from the south it blows the bait into the fish's mouth.' We get the beautiful south wind that we wait for in the spring," Redbird said, adding, "And we can't get it too soon after we've had that severe, cold winter. We now salute the south wind."

"Salute," all the hobos repeated.

"Third, we will salute the east wind." Double B took the fusee and pointed with it to the east. The hobos all turned to the east, raising their sticks in the new direction.

"The east wind is not the best, but we still need it," Redbird said. "An old saying goes like this: 'When the wind is from the east, it's neither good for man nor beast.' We salute the eastern winds because they have some use. We now salute the eastern winds."

"Salute," the other hobos echoed.

"And last, we will salute the west winds." Adman took the flare from Double B and turned to the west. He wore a leather bucket hat with a long animal tail attached to it. Behind him, the fire crackled energetically, sending up tongues of flame. The crowd whispered nervously, watching the flames get dangerously close to Adman's adopted tail. Adman sensed the heat and took a couple of steps forward, away from the fire, and the crowd relaxed. The hobos picked up their sticks and pointed them to the west.

Redbird went on, "Another old saying goes: 'When the wind is from the west, it is time for the very best.' We get that beautiful sunset in the west, and that's also where we get our rain. The rain from the west brings moisture to our crops and makes everything grow. We will now salute the west winds."

"Salute." The hobos saluted as before.

"That's the wind ceremony we go through every year," Redbird said to the crowd. "These words are from Frisco Jack. I had permission from Frisco Jack before he passed away last year to use these words. I've been using them for about 15 years now, I guess."

The fire burned hot, its orange flames adding to the August heat.

The Ashes Ceremony

Redbird directed a new question to the hobos: "Does anybody have ashes to dump in the fire?"

For a moment, I wondered if I had heard him correctly. He wanted people to dump ashes *into* the fire? In answer to Redbird's question, many hobos moved to an area at the side of the fire. Each one who stepped into the orderly line carried a cup or a jar of some kind. As the ceremony proceeded, I learned that their containers held ashes from other hobo gatherings or home fires, and this was another tradition that connected the hobo community.

Medicine Man was the first to come to the fire. He dumped the contents of his container into the fire. "From Rochelle, Illinois, and return to Britt," he said.

"Who's next with ashes?" Redbird asked.

Iwegan came forward, emptying his cup into the fire. "Ashes from Road Hog USA," he said.

"We buried him today out here at the National Hobo Cemetery," Redbird told the spectators.

But only some of him, I thought, remembering that at the cemetery, small bags of ashes were available to anyone who wanted them. Iwegan contributed his bag of Road Hog USA's ashes to the hobo campfire tradition; others would see to it that the wind would further Road Hog's travels.

Dante, the hobo who had represented the south wind, was next.

"You've got a lot of ashes to dump," Redbird remarked. "Dante is our current Hobo King," Redbird told the spectators. The other hobos cheered. "Where are your ashes from?"

Dante emptied a steady stream of ashes onto the fire. "Kansas City, Minnesota, and Britt," he answered.

One by one, other hobos stepped forward, adding a bit of history to the fire as they told the source of their ashes.

"From home fires and the brothers and sisters that have gone before us," Adman said.

"Plymouth, Connecticut," Slim Tim said.

"From the Connecticut gathering, my home fire at Abbott Village, Maine, and some from Britt last year," said Lady Nightingale, one of the Serenity singers.

"From the fire pit in our back yard." said another hobo.

"From Britt last year, and from my home fire in Dexter, Maine."

"From different places in Minneapolis, Minnesota, and from Minneapolis Jewel's house. She had a hobo gathering and we had a great time."

"Deep Lock Quarry Days in Peninsula, Ohio."

A hobo called Half Track came forward. "From my home fire in Minnesota, from Minneapolis, and Britt," she said. "And a little preacher. Preacher Steve—he always comes back."

Wingnut was the last hobo with ashes. "From Britt, Iowa, and Road Hog. A little bit of Road Hog going in here," he said.

The last bits of ashes had been added, and the campfire ceremonies were complete, but the evening's activities, billed as the "Night of 1000 Stars," were just starting. In the hobo tradition, the hobos would entertain each other and jungle visitors with music, dance, and poetry—a testament to their talents, creativity, patriotism, and sense of community.

THE NIGHT OF 1,000 STARS: HOBO ENTERTAINMENT

Redbird turned the microphone over to the current Hobo Queen, Double B, who lives in Pennsylvania, and Dante, the current Hobo King, who lives in Minnesota.

Double B spoke first. She wore a straw hat, a blue shirt, and a skirt that extended from an Oshkosh overall top all the way to the ground. "This is very close to the end of my reign, and I want to tell everyone that I had a wonderful, wonderful year. I did manage to get to some of the other gatherings. I tried to keep in touch with Dante, but he's a hard man to get a hold of." The hobos laughed; perhaps when the wanderlust hits, all the hobos are hard to track down, I thought. Double B continued, "Everywhere I went, [Dante] was asked about, and he went to some places that I didn't...

"I love the people of Britt and my hobo family... I hope whoever succeeds me will have every bit as good a year," she finished.

Then it was Dante's turn. "She's far more eloquent than I am, so whatever she says has to be right." The crowd laughed, and Dante, not wanting to give a speech, added simply, "That's my story and I'm sticking to it," and he turned over the mic to Medicine Man, who was the night's emcee.

The evening's entertainment opened with the national anthem, sung a capella and in tuneful three-part harmony by the Serenity singers, composed of three hobo women: Lady Nightingale, Blue Moon Bo, and Lady Sonshine, who dedicated their performance to our military. "Not only the ones in Afghanistan," Lady Nightingale said, "but everywhere we have sent them out to... Freedom doesn't come free."

They sang all three verses of the "Star Spangled Banner," which is their tradition, as I would learn over the next few days. Anytime the anthem was sung during the activities at the convention—and it was sung often— the Serenity singers were the ones to lead the singing, and they proudly sang three verses, except once, at the start of the ceremony to elect the Hobo King and Queen, when they were asked to sing only one verse. They begrudgingly complied, but not without showing their disapproval.

Three verses. I certainly didn't know all the words, and I'm betting most people don't know them, either. I looked it up later, and to my surprise, there are *four* verses. I'm sure if the Serenity singers find that fourth verse, they'll add it to their performances. For the record, and so that no one has to go look it up, here are the verses:

O! say can you see by the dawn's early light,
What so proudly we hailed at the twilight's last gleaming,
Whose broad stripes and bright stars through the perilous fight,
O'er the ramparts we watched, were so gallantly streaming?
And the rockets' red glare, the bombs bursting in air,
Gave proof through the night that our flag was still there;
O! say does that star-spangled banner yet wave,
O'er the land of the free and the home of the brave?

On the shore dimly seen through the mists of the deep,
Where the foe's haughty host in dread silence reposes,
What is that which the breeze, o'er the towering steep,
As it fitfully blows, half conceals, half discloses?
Now it catches the gleam of the morning's first beam,
In full glory reflected now shines in the stream:
'Tis the star-spangled banner, O! long may it wave
O'er the land of the free and the home of the brave.

And where is that band who so vauntingly swore
That the havoc of war and the battle's confusion,
A home and a country, should leave us no more?
Their blood has washed out their foul footsteps' pollution.
No refuge could save the hireling and slave
From the terror of flight, or the gloom of the grave:
And the star-spangled banner in triumph doth wave,
O'er the land of the free and the home of the brave.

O! thus be it ever, when freemen shall stand
Between their loved home and the war's desolation.
Blest with vict'ry and peace, may the Heav'n rescued land
Praise the Power that hath made and preserved us a nation!
Then conquer we must, when our cause it is just,
And this be our motto: "In God is our trust;"
And the star-spangled banner in triumph shall wave
O'er the land of the free and the home of the brave!

The Night of 1000 Stars was a kind of mulligan stew that simmered with talents of all kinds and levels. It made me think of the hobo tradition in the jungle, where it's a matter of pride for each hobo to contribute something to the stew.

Some hobos kept their contribution as simple as an announcement: Collinwood Kid, wearing a Dumpster Diving Team T-shirt, asked for address updates from anyone in the hobo community "who considers themselves part of our family." Later, he would compile an updated list that could be purchased for one dollar—a contribution to his "toner, paper, and gas-to-go-home fund."

He was followed by "Pineapple" Jack and Birdman, playing "Honolulu Baby" on ukulele and a one-man percussion stick decorated with a Tourist Union 63 sticker pasted on a cymbal. Minneapolis Jewel, wearing a flower in her hair, two leis over a black bra, and a long grass skirt over her short denim skirt, danced the hula. Iwegan, wearing a red bandana, a leather vest, and denim shorts, gamely took Jewel's hand and danced with her.

Luther the Jet, standing tall in camouflage pants and a Led Zeppelin "Hammer of the Gods" T-shirt, told of going to Newfoundland in 1977 to ride a famous train called the Bullet. "Way, way out there on the edge of the world," Luther said. The line was all curves—no straight track, which Luther included in his original song titled the "Newfie Bullet." The song began this way:

In 500 miles of curving track
No tunnel could be found
No obstacle was small enough
It couldn't be gone around

And with those curves
There oft appeared
A long and steep incline
For hillsides were our specialty
Along the Newfie line

Lonnie, a hobo with Native American heritage, was up next. She brought her native flute, but apologized in advance to the crowd, explaining that she was hindered by COPD. She dedicated her song, called "Sweet Child," to those who had caught the Westbound. She played her flute despite a missing middle and index finger on her left hand which, amazingly enough, seemed to barely hinder her.

Medicine Man, who had taken over the emcee duties, called for a dance known as the "hobo shuffle." He invited everyone to dance around the campfire and asked people to "dig in their pockets and put some money into the hats that will be going around. It's how we pay our musicians."

Lady Sonshine stepped up to the microphone with her guitar in hand and launched into an energetic performance of "Johnny Be Good." Frog, maneuvering his wheelchair, was one of the first hobos to enter the shuffle. A little red-haired girl, an honorary hobo, joined him, and they sang along as they danced. Many hobos and a few spectators circled the fire, stepping lively in pairs or kicking up their heels solo, and on the perimeter, several people passed hats and collected contributions.

The evening's stew continued with Grandpa and M.A.D. Mary, who waved American flags and sang their version of "I'm Just a Flag-Waving American." Grandpa held a flag in one hand and steadied himself with his hobo walking stick in the other, and when they finished singing together, Grandpa started chanting his own song, a true story about a train derailment, called "The Train Ride to Nowhere." (See Grandpa's interview for the lyrics.)

Next, Hobo Jack, a gaunt old hobo with long gray hair and a full gray beard extending to the middle of his chest, settled onto a metal chair in front of the microphone and sang "Railroad Bill" and "Cripple Creek" while accompanying himself on his banjo.

He switched to guitar—an old, beat up instrument with rippled and split veneer—and added a harmonica and holder around his neck, Dylan style. He played his own composition called "Freight Train Whistle Blues," a song about freight trains, picking fruit in many states, and about lost loves:

If you ever have to hop a freight train
Cause a woman done let you go
Just get on tracks in some country town
And learn what the rest of us know

Freight train whistle blues
Freight train whistle blues
The music of that whistle going 'round in my head
Till I'm layin' in my grave cold and stone dead.

A tall, thin hobo dressed simply in a dark shirt, dark pants, and dark baseball cap came to the mic. His name was Roadkill, and he started his contribution in the manner of Garrison Keillor: "This program is brought to you by the Road Kill Café, famous for its carrion… and carry-out. You kill it, we grill it. This program is also brought to you by the Northern States Railroad, serving northern Iowa hobos since 1877. The 'no bull' railroad."

Referring to his notes from time to time, Roadkill recited two poems by Scottish poet Robert Service. The first was called "The Men Who Don't Fit In." One of the stanzas seemed to aptly describe the hobos:

He is one of the Legion Lost;
He was never meant to win;
He's a rolling stone, and it's bred in the bone;
He's a man who can't fit in.

The second poem, titled "Bindle Stiff," contained a verse that probably explained why Roadkill was dressed the way he was:

And as I tramped the railway track
I owned a single shirt;
Like a canny Scot I bought it black
So's not to show the dirt.

As the evening's shadows lengthened, more music followed, including a song written by Rambling Rudy, an old hobo who had caught the Westbound many years ago; a song called "Music in My Mother's House," performed in a clear, true voice by Sunrise; and old folk songs, like "Five Hundred Miles." And the campfire burned on, fuel for the mulligan of talent the hobos shared .

The previous year's Hobo King and Queen have a seat of honor on the hobo float.

FIRST THE PARADE, THEN THE MULLIGAN

On Saturday morning of the National Hobo Convention, people gathered early on the streets of Britt, positioning camp chairs and blankets curbside to secure a good spot for viewing the Hobo Days Parade. The savory aroma of mulligan wafted over the area from the town park as a crew of volunteers stirred the gallons of stew simmering in rows of large drums.

Many people had tucked containers of all kinds under their chairs: Rubbermaid and Tupperware storage dishes in all shapes and sizes, some pots and pans, and even a few metal Dutch ovens with lids. My husband turned to me and said, "They must throw a lot of candy in this parade!"

At 10 o'clock, the parade began, led by the VFW post bearing a sign acknowledging the service of all veterans. Next came a float starring the hobos. Last year's National Hobo King and Queen sat up high, perched on a raised platform—their seat of honor—waving to the crowd. This was the last morning of their reign, because a new King and Queen would be elected this afternoon. All kinds of floats and vehicles followed—from old fire trucks to antique cars to tractors pulling floats sponsored by real estate agencies, insurance companies, health care businesses, and churches. Everyone seemed to be throwing candy; the spectators—especially the kids—scrambled to catch it, but no one appeared to be depositing the candy in their containers.

High school marching bands punctuated the parade flow with music, and the Shriners ran their group of bright red, highly polished little cars in orchestrated patterns on the street. Finally, at nearly noon, the last float passed by and the horses arrived, signaling the end of the parade.

The announcer invited everyone to come partake of the mulligan. A long line formed on the sidewalk as hobos, townspeople, and visitors waited together to receive a generous bowl of stew. After everyone had been served, the announcer took the microphone again and encouraged anyone who had a container to come get more stew to take home. Aha! Jim and I nodded at each other. This solved the mystery of the pots, pans, and plastic dishes.

Volunteers make enough mulligan to serve 5,000. They use twenty 55-gallon containers. The cooking is supervised by Dwight Leerar. The Catholic Church youth group cuts the veggies, and the After Prom committee serves it after the coronation.

Mulligan Stew Recipe for Britt, Iowa

450 lbs. of meat	100 lbs. of turnips
900 lbs. of potatoes	10 lbs. of parsnips
250 lbs. of carrots	150 lbs. of tomatoes
300 lbs. of cabbage	25 lbs. rice
24 gallons of mixed vegetables	20 lbs. chili pepper
	Salt, pepper, and other seasonings

Next, hobos and several Britt officials gathered in the gazebo to prepare for the election of the National Hobo King and Queen. The hobos, many dressed in denim and wearing bandanas and hats decorated with buttons and patches from their travels, seated themselves on several rows of folding chairs. The front row was reserved for last year's Hobo King and Queen and those who are running this year. Candidates glanced nervously at the papers in their hands as they prepared to give their speech.

KING AND QUEEN
FESTIVITIES IN THE GAZEBO

As the festivities began, the mayor introduced the Serenity singers, who would sing the "Star Spangled Banner." The three women stepped up to the mic. "We have been *requested* to sing only one verse," said one of the members, clearly not in agreement with the decision. Another member stepped up. "So you get to choose which verse!" she said, brightly. Then they launched, a capella, into the first verse, which is the one everybody knows.

Two of the three singers sat down after the national anthem, and the third, Blue Moon Bo, who is also the violin player for the group and daughter of a hobo, stayed to speak. She was tall and slender with long brown hair. Although it was a very warm day, she was wearing a black long-sleeved sweater and a denim vest.

BLUE MOON BO: Greetings, Britt. Back in 1991 when I first started coming here with my Dad, Fishbones, I really didn't know what to expect with all of his friends, but I got to meet a lot of the old 'bo's. And every year it seems like the page has turned in the hobo history. We have lost so many people this year.

When 1993 rolled around, I decided I was running for Queen. Of course, that was the year you had all the flooding out here, and my dad and I discussed whether or not we actually should come. You had so much trouble out here, we didn't want to be a burden to people. So we called up Harold and said, Gee, we don't think that we should come this year—it seems like you've had enough trouble and you don't need us."

And he said, "No, no, you need to come. All the hobos need to come because we need cheering up out here."

And so we did come. And I decided to run for Queen, and lo and behold, Blackie decided to run, again, for King. He had never been King. He was a hometown boy and he wanted to be King desperately. So he was always promoting himself. Last year, he was sitting right down there [she points at a spot in the crowd], promoting himself, as always, with his books, and I got to meet Blackie.

I think my most favorite memory of him is…Sunday morning they used to have… a poetry reading. I know Slim was there. But there was a bunch of people there, and the poem [Blackie] recited that people like the most was "The Diarrhea Poem." If you've never read that, you've got to read that. I never laughed so hard in my life. So he decided he was running for King, and I said I was running for Queen, although I didn't know much about it. And the only one that opposed me was Slo Freight Ben…everybody else stepped back. So I recited my poem for the event. I was going to play a fiddle tune, but it was so blasted hot after the rain it was like being in a very big sauna, and I wasn't used to it. So I said I'm going to write a poem about your stew. Your stew is really good. I had never had it, although people were telling me I should try some of that stuff. But it was too hot and I couldn't stand the thought of eating things hot because that would have made me sick. So I wrote this poem:

There's a town in the west
Where they say there's the best
Hobo stew made in that town named Britt
In August each year
Folks travel there so I hear
Just to eat that hot stuff—Imagine it
We eat stew if the weather's hot
I rather think not
That task is for souls braver than I
But I'm told all true hobos should try
They say it's quite tasty and here's why
The good folks of Britt
All quietly sit
For hours just making the stuff
Peeling carrots and spuds

And veggies by the tubs
Until someone shouts, "Stop—that's enough!"
Then thousands of gallons of stew start to cook
And in that heat I'll bet those stirrers do, too
Just so folks from away
Come hobo day
Can get it for free—oh, believe me it's true
Thousands of men, women, and children
All shapes and sizes
Patiently waiting their turns
To hold out a cup or a pan to fill up
While overhead the sun burns and burns
Dedication, that's what it's called
Why else would any sane person stand
Out on those streets
In that sweltering heat
To get some hot stew in a can
Eat hobo stew while the weather's hot—
Oh, I rather think not
My stomach recoils at that thought
My New England blood would just turn to mud
At the folly my stomach had wrought
So I just sit in the shade
With my cold lemonade
And smile as they slowly march by
And think of cold things
And the chill that they bring
While the sun burns and burns in the sky

So that was my poem, and then when Blackie got to be King—after I was announced Queen—he wanted it so bad, he broke down and started crying. And I think he was feeling a little bit embarrassed, so I said, "Blackie, come on. I'm not that bad."

The crowd laughed, and she handed the mic to an old hobo named Grandpa, who addressed the crowd in a thready, quavery voice. He sported a gray beard and moustache and wore a black hat with a yellow hatband that read Hobo King 2001.

GRANDPA: Hello. I am a former resident of Britt. I lived here in the '30s, and I can remember some of the old hobos. This year has become one of the greatest, as far as I'm concerned. We have a good fellowship, I've met some good people here, and it's great being here. I ran for King of the Hobos in 2001 and you people made me King. I appreciate that very much. It's an awesome thing, really. It's a national office, you know. We try to go to every gathering we can. We come to Britt if we possibly can. We come every year. It's just great. ... I hope you use good judgment in who you're voting for—I'm sure you will. I have nothing more to say, I'm just extremely happy to be here.

Luther the Jet was up next. The emcee introduced him, saying, "Now we'll hear from Luther the Jet....I have no idea what he's going to do, because you don't know him." Luther stepped up to the mic, laughing along with the crowd. Over a black T-shirt, he wore a plaid flannel shirt with the sleeves cut off, making it more of a vest. He was tall, slender, with a brown beard and moustache, and he leaned on a walking stick as he addressed the crowd.

LUTHER: [laughs] We'll just make it up as we go along.... I've lived in Madison, Wisconsin for quite a while, and everybody here I'm sure has heard the name Scott Walker, who got himself elected governor of Wisconsin last year *[some of the crowd boos]* and immediately started raising a ruckus over there by trying to take away the collective bargaining rights of the public employees' union. So the People's Republic of Madison got up in arms about that, and I went up and resurrected a few of the great old labor tunes to sing. There were a lot of people up there from all around the country at the state capitol in Madison. One day when it was real cold, I could only sing one song at a time before I was freezing my butt off. I sang that great old "Joe Hill" song. I adjusted it a little bit for local circumstances. So I would like to do that.

Ninety-nine years old this song is. It was written for a strike on the Canadian-Northern Railway in 1912 by the immortal Joe Hill.

Hello, hobos, pay attention
A few facts I will mention
About the fixed intention
Of the workers of the world.
And I hope you'll all be ready
Bravehearted true and steady
And rally 'round the banner
When the union flags unfurl

Where the old Yahara flows
Each union worker knows
They've bullied and oppressed us
But still our union grows
And we're gonna find a way now
To bargain for our pay now
And we're gonna win the day now
Where the old Yahara flows

Oh, Scott Walker, the law he's stretchin'
The pimps and goons he's fetchin'
And they're a fine collection
As Jesus only knows
But why their mothers reared them
Or why the devil's spared them
Are questions we can't answer
Where the old Yahara flows

Where the old Yahara flows
Each union worker knows
They've bullied and oppressed us

But still our union grows
And we're gonna find a way now
To bargain for our pay now
And we're gonna win the day now
Where the old Yahara flows

Oh these David Koch contactors
They're mean and dirty actors
They're not our benefactors
As every worker knows
So we've got to stick together
Through fine or stormy weather
We'll show them no white feather
Where the old Yahara flows

Fellow hobos, thank you for your attention.
A few facts I have mentioned
About the fixed intention of the workers of the world
And I hope you'll all be ready
Brave-hearted, true, and steady
And rally 'round the banner when the union flags unfurl

Double B, last year's Hobo Queen, took her turn to speak.

DOUBLE B: I just want to thank everyone for electing me last year as national hobo Queen. I have had a great year. I've visited four or five gatherings. We dubbed ten people, and I've given at least ten talks. Some of them Redbird Express and I worked together. It's been a wonderful year and I've met so many wonderful people. Whenever I speak about the hobos, it doesn't come without speaking about Britt, and how wonderful the town is, and it makes it so wonderful to come back. I hope that whoever is Queen next year will have a year every bit as good as I've had.

Dante, last year's Hobo King, gave the shortest speech of the day.

DANTE: I've learned the best lesson in life: let the women do the speaking for you. Thank you very much.

He stepped away and the delighted crowd applauded enthusiastically. Minneapolis Jewel, Hobo Queen in 1986, 1981, and 1997, then came to the mic. Her bright yellow shirt contrasted with her denim overalls, and she wore a straw hat with red flowers and a raccoon tail that made me think of Daniel Boone.

MINNEAPOLIS JEWEL: Hi Everybody. I'm laughing right now, but I really want to tell you my heart is so, so broken over the loss of three very important and close hobos to me: Road Hog USA, Railroad Randy, who was from Minneapolis, who came to my home several times for gatherings and parties in the back yard, and Iowa Blackie, who I've known for 32 years, and I want to tell you Blackie right now, I did love you in my own way. Just for the record…I just wanted to acknowledge those three, and I see Railroad Randy's brother, Tim, here. Frog, my King from 1997, who went from Montana down to Reno, Nevada, with his own handicaps and difficulties, and picked up the ashes of Road Hog and made sure they came to Britt.

…In the last year I had a stroke, which is a serious medical [issue]…. But I personally want to thank some people for helping me through a hard time and being there. C'mon Pat…she was a big help to me…and Frog, who moved from Montana to Minneapolis. He got himself in a kettle of fish, but he has been helping at my home so much. Frog I can't even begin to thank you. I know like a good hobo you're going to be gone in the spring, and that's fine, but I want to thank you now.

She thanked a host of other hobos for their help in her recovery: Uncle Freddie, Shorty and Maggie, James Pied Piper, Trucker Phil, Lady Nightingale, and Jewel's husband, Tuck. She ended by saying:

JEWEL: I want to thank Cannonball Paul, Bonnie Bookworm, and Birdman, who now goes by Gilligan, for making me get up [she starts to laugh] and do the hula dance in the show on Thursday.

Again, the Serenity singers gathered at the microphone. One of the women introduced their next song:

LADY NIGHTINGALE: Ramblin' Rudy wrote this about himself. It's a poem he put on the back of a book he authored, and we put some music to it. It tells about his life on the road.

He's just an old hobo who rode the rails
And did time in many a dirty jail
For reaching his way down the vagabond trail
Listening to the freight train's lonely wail
He's rode every railroad in this land
From Portland, Maine, to the Rio Grande
Across the burning desert with blowing sand
And he took it all just like a man, yes he took it all just like a man

He was always broke, and hungry, too
He had seen all the sights and scenic views
Sometimes happy just singing the blues
After eating that hobo mulligan stew

He has slept on the ground many a time
For he did not have even a dime
Knocked on back doors with the same old line
Asking for a handout with a hungry whine

He has sailed the seas and even stowed away
And was a hobo delegate out in Britt, I–O Way
Tried for King of Hobos on election day
Like a hobo, he loves the good old USA

Ramblin' Rudy would some day be heavenbound
Riding that glory train with musical sounds
His sins all forgiven and peace he has found
His final ride will be to westward near Johnny town

He has rode every railroad in this land
From Portland, Maine, to the Rio Grande
Across the burning desert with blowing sand
And he took it all just like a man, yes he took it all just like a man

The hobo named Adman spoke next. He spoke very hesitantly and paused to search for words.

ADMAN: People are hurting. A lot of people. We're losing our middle class. The hobos aren't the only ones, and what I wanted to talk about is that the hobo family is kind of weaving together by looking at society from the outside in. A favor, a gift is if you see somebody, look them in the eye, because no one ever does… These times and in hobos' times. The fact is we all matter. We all matter.

This is my thirty-ninth year of riding freight trains, and I think I'll run for Hobo King next year.

An elderly black woman wearing a bandana stepped up. She is referred to more simply as Hobo Lump, and she was elected Queen in 1981, 1983, and 1987. ("Lump" is a hobo term for a handout of a meal.)

EMPRESS VAGABOND HOBO LUMP: Hi everyone. I've been coming here 30 years now, and I've enjoyed myself, I've been your hobo Queen three times, and now they made me Empress Vagabond of the Third World. … But I like this town so much that I'm becoming a neighbor of Britt. [*The crowd applauded and hooted.*] The Britt Creamery is going to be my retreat, and I'm going to enjoy it as is, and I'm going to have to take it piece by piece, but I hope I'll be a good neighbor to Britt.

Two more hobos followed, each wanting to address the crowd and their friends.

SUNRISE: This is my tenth anniversary coming here, and I almost didn't make it because my van, my good old Volkswagen van, broke down in Galena, Illinois, and my friend Max, who was leaning upon a tree out there somewhere…I just wanted to say thank you to Max for coming to get me and bringing me to Britt. This is where I needed to be. I love you.

VIRGINIA SLIM: I've only been coming here 40 years. In 1971 I wandered in. I've probably garnered a few stories. My wife, Kathy, said, "If you don't get up and sing a song for Ann Hagan, you ain't going home in that truck."

He took a deep breath and began to sing; his voice was a rich baritone that was right on pitch.

I've been working in the Army
I've been working on the farm
All I've got to show is the muscle in my arm
And it looks like I'm never gonna cease my wanderin'

I've been travelin' early
I've been travelin' late
From New York City out to the Golden Gate
And it looks like I'm never gonna cease my wanderin'

The bright stars up above me
The green grass on the ground
I've been searching for something I have never found
And it looks like I'm never gonna cease my wanderin'

Well, it's ashes to ashes
It's dust unto dust
If the railroad doesn't get you then the breadlines must
And it looks like I'm never gonna cease my wanderin'

THE KING AND QUEEN ELECTION AND CORONATION

Everyone who wanted to speak had an opportunity, so the election of the King and Queen began. First were candidates for Queen. Each person had two minutes to give a campaign speech, and when all the candidates for Queen have spoken, a vote would be taken by applause.

There were four candidates: Sunflower, Minneapolis Jewel, M.A.D. Mary, and Cookin' Mama. A young, blonde-haired woman named Sunflower was the first to speak. She wore faded jeans, a pink and blue tie-dyed shirt, and a red bandana. She seemed a little nervous, but she bravely addressed the crowd, reading from her notes.

SUNFLOWER: Hello, Britt. It's good to be home. I've grown up here most all my life. It was Wingnut that lured me to the road a year ago during these great Hobo Days. It's been great riding the rails, working, utilizing my artistic talents to ride again…to feel and experience scenery that can only be experienced from riding the freights. During our travels, Bill and I developed the kind of relationship that can only be expressed fully tonight in the jungle, where we will vow to commit the entirety of our lives together. As a Hobo Queen, I will dedicate to the cause of telling people of our great town Britt, and the honorable hobos who come to gather here. So I hope to see you all at the jungle tonight as your Queen, so for now, may we meet, may we part, and may we meet again.

Jewel took her turn. She stepped up to the front of the gazebo with confidence and spoke to the crowd in an assured voice that carried so well she probably didn't need the microphone.

JEWEL: I have my top 10 list … top 10 reasons why I should be this year's Hobo Queen:

10. Because I've been coming to Britt for 32 consecutive years.

9. Because I feed the hobos and tramps that come to my house. And also some of the neighborhood bums, but I love them, too.

8. I put my whole heart into keeping the hobo family alive, and their history.

7. I haven't been Queen yet in this century.

6. Because I rode freight trains through Iowa with Iowa Blackie in 1991 for a couple of weeks, and that was quite an experience.

5. Because I correspond the old-fashioned way. I write letters to people.

4. I live the hobo philosophy every day.

3. I throw great hobo parties.

2. I always try to find the goodness in people.

1. And the number 1 reason I should be this year's Hobo Queen is....badadadadada...drum roll...because I'm married to Tuck!

The crowd cheered appreciatively, and Jewel looked out to where Tuck was standing. "I love ya, honey!" she said as she moved to return to her seat.

The third candidate was M.A.D. Mary. She was dressed all in blue: blue jeans, a blue blouse, and a blue vest. Her hair was gray and curly and was cropped very short. She was a quiet woman, but came to the mic with poise.

M.A.D. MARY: I remember in 1997 when I got up here, I was shaking, and I was really nervous. Then I found that the people in Britt are the most wonderful people in the world. And I love the hobos, and I have found this year that more than ever, that the hobos are loving people, and they care for each other and care for me. So I'd really like to be their Queen.

I was Queen in 2000, and have, since then, traveled all over the country and everywhere we go, the hobos are shared. We tell them about the hobos in Britt and how wonderful they are, and that's not going to stop.

So I would really like to be the Queen of the hobos this year, and I will keep getting out the history of the hobos and meeting with them whenever there's a chance.

The last candidate to speak was Cookin' Mama. She, too, was dressed in denim.

COOKIN' MAMA: I'm from Galesburg, Illinois. I'd love to be your national Hobo Queen. I've been your crumb boss down at the jungle several times. I've hosted a hobo gathering in Galesburg, Illinois, two years and that's how I met the hobos. They've stayed at my house. I've cooked for them—that's why I'm Cookin' Mama, and it led me to Britt.

I'm a rubber tramp hobo. I travel for my work, seeking out other hobos, asking 'Do you go to Britt? Do you know about Britt?' There's a lot of people that don't. I would love to represent Britt as your Hobo Queen, to tell the history of Britt and the hobos. Elect me, Cookin' Mama, as your Queen, and I'll come back next year to Britt with great stories to tell of my life on the road as your Hobo Queen. Thank you and God Bless.

The announcer explained that now each Queen candidate would return to the gazebo stage, and the crowd should applaud for the one they want to be Queen. "Spotters" were stationed at several places within the audience to gauge the level of applause in each area. One by one, each Queen candidate heard her applause. Disappointment registered on several faces as they realized the applause was not enough. The announcer conferred with the spotters and then returned to the gazebo.

"Now I know who the Queen is," he said, "and now we'll go to the election of the King."

A young man named Wingnut took his turn. He was young and tanned, with dark hair and a dark, neatly trimmed beard. He was dressed simply in faded blue jeans, a gray sleeveless muscle shirt, and a black and gray bandana. I recognized him because over the past two days, he and his bride-to-be, Sunflower, had been campaigning in the jungle, carrying signs with elaborate and colorful writing: Please Elect Sunflower for Hobo Queen said one sign, with the last "O" in hobo turned into a red polka-dotted bindle. Please Elect Wingnut 4 Hobo King, said the other. The words Still Ridin had been added at the bottom, and the "ng" in Wingnut's name descended into railroad tracks.

WINGNUT: Hello, Britt, Iowa. My name is Wingnut. I've been riding freight trains for ten years. This is my third year here in Britt, Iowa. I came here in 2009, rode a train into Mason City, hitched the rest of the way into here, and met the love of my life. Sunflower. In 2010 I came back, left again, to hit the rails again. I asked her to ride with me, and she did. And I thank God for that. I thank Britt for having us here—to have one of your own riding with me on the rails. I believe Britt, Iowa, deserves to have an active, train-riding hobo as King. Thank you.

The second candidate for King was Uncle Freddie. He is known as a "bridger"—a hobo who has ridden both steam and diesel.

UNCLE FREDDIE: Hello, everyone...Well, who'll tell the stories of the past? Wood floors in the boxcars, the clickety-clack of the rails as they were all bolted down...the waterholes, the caboose, the gandy dancers, the jungles as they used to be... All these things, if you would like to know, will always be here in Britt, at least once a year. So while you are here, enjoy all the tales and the stories of the years gone by. Never forget the hobos. They will always show up in Britt for the convention. And I pray [for] and thank all the women and men in the armed forces that give us the privilege to be here today. Freedom is not free. Take a moment and just think about it. God bless you, and God bless America. Thank you.

Uncle Freddie took his seat and the announcer called several times for the third candidate. No one came up, so he finally called for the vote. First was the applause for Wingnut. The crowd was very enthusiastic. Next was the applause for Uncle Freddie. The crowd was equally enthusiastic, but I noticed there was extended time for Freddie's applause.

Again the announcer conferred with the spotters while the crowd waited. He came back to the microphone and declared Minneapolis Jewel and Uncle

Freddie to be the new Queen and King. Two capes —blue with white trim for the Queen and red with white trim for the King—were brought onstage and draped over Jewel and Freddie's shoulders. Finally, they were crowned with straw hats topped with Folgers coffee cans cut in the zigzag shape of a royal crown and trimmed with red bandanas.

The crowd applauded madly; Jewel thanked everybody, and Uncle Freddie declared himself speechless.

Uncle Freddie and Minneapolis Jewel, the newly elected Hobo King and Queen.

Sunflower and Wingnut throw rhubarb leaves into the fire during the wedding ceremony.

Saturday evening, after the parade, the mulligan, the coronation of the King and Queen ,and other festivities, people were invited to witness a hobo wedding in the jungle.

IN GENTLE KINDNESS:
THE HOBO WEDDING

The bride wore a creamy white strapless wedding gown with a lightly beaded, embroidered bodice and a flowing skirt. Her upswept hair, a cascade of light brown and blonde streaked curls, was anchored with a glittery tiara and two sunflowers. Now and then, the late afternoon sun caught the stud above her upper lip, sending out a quick spark of light, and when she turned away from the crowd, I could see the tattoo above her shoulder blades, although I couldn't decipher it. It seemed slightly out of focus.

The groom was dressed in a light yellow shirt under fresh, railroad-striped blue overalls that hung nicely on his trim frame. Around his neck was a neatly knotted red bandana, with a button reading Got Hobos? pinned through the knot. He sported a pristine pork pie hat with a cigarette tucked into the band. At the last minute, he had selected that hat over a well-worn Australian-style hat, one that by the looks of it had been a favorite. His round glasses gave him a rather dapper appearance, and he exuded energy and a bit of nervousness.

The guests—a mix of townspeople, hobos, and convention goers—sat on two small sets of bleachers positioned for a good view of the campfire, which had been recently stoked. It crackled, sending off a few swirls of smoke and adding to the summer heat. Some of the overflow crowd set up camp chairs or sat in the grass. Some just milled aimlessly, cameras in hand, waiting for the scheduled activity to begin. In the early evening of Saturday, August 13, Sunflower and Wingnut, the bride and groom, probably in their early 20s, were about to be married in the jungle.

To start the ceremony, about eighteen or twenty hobos formed two rows at one side of the campfire and turned to face each other. Their manner of dress was much more informal than the bride and groom's. Luther the Jet was a tall presence in his camouflage pants and a plaid, sleeveless shirt. Denim was everywhere—C'mon Pat wore a denim shirt with her name embroidered on a patch on the back. Connecticut Shorty and New York Maggie—two sisters who had spent sixteen years living and traveling across the country together in a 26-foot camper—wore denim vests thick with embroidered patches from their travels. Many of the men wore blue jeans and t-shirts. Some wore railroad caps.

At a signal, the hobos who were lined up lifted their walking sticks and crossed them, forming an arch. A guitarist, a friend of the bride and groom, played an instrumental piece he had composed to accompany the bride as she walked under the arch toward the shade of the large tree where the service would be performed. She carried a bouquet of black-eyed Susans accented with lavender and purple wildflowers, following the hobo tradition of carrying wildflowers that can be found along the railroad tracks—there is rarely money available to purchase flowers.

I knew that inside the bouquet, a hobo named M.A.D Mary had tucked several thistles, another hobo tradition intended to be a reality check. Earlier, she had explained their significance to me. "In addition to being beautiful, marriage can also be prickly," she said. "It's a reminder."

Wingnut joined Sunflower under the tree, and Black Knight, wearing dark pants and a black t-shirt that befitted his name, stood nearby, ready to officiate. His salt-and-pepper hair, full beard, and moustache were neatly trimmed. He wore a black fedora hat, stylishly tilted, and a silver necklace with HOBO KING spelled out in silver beads. He stepped up to the mic and looked out at the spectators, "We are doing this ceremony because Sunflower and Wingnut have chosen to be married in the hobo jungle. This is something that they should cherish for life, and the vows are not to be taken lightly." He turned to Wingnut and asked, "Do you understand that?"

"Yes," Wingnut answered.

Black Knight turned to Sunflower. "Do you understand that?"

"Yes," she said.

Clearly, Black Knight was serious about his role, as well. He took control of the ceremony with quiet authority.

He called for rhubarb; there was a bit of confusion, a brief flurry of activity, and a momentary pause in the ceremony while the plants were located. After a few minutes, someone hurried in with two stalks of rhubarb, and the bride and groom were each given one. "This symbolizes severing all your ties to any evil that you might be doing, and not taking it into your wedding with you," Black Knight said to them. Wingnut and Sunflower walked around the campfire, tearing pieces of the leaves off the stalk and throwing the leaves into the fire. Because the leaves are poisonous, Black Knight explained, burning them represents destroying the bad parts of the relationship. They keep the stalk because it's food—and it is especially good with strawberries in pie, Black Knight suggested. The fruit also represents food for the marriage.

While the bride and groom performed this ritual, the Serenity singers began singing a song adapted especially for the occasion: *We're goin' to the jungle and we're goin' to get married....goin' to the jungle of love,* they harmonized to the tune of "Chapel of Love."

Next, Black Knight announced, Sunflower and Wingnut will circle the fire in a celebratory dance, and he invited the audience to join in. He introduced one of the Serenity singers, Lady Sonshine, who stepped up to the mic and said, "And it's not a waltz, either." She grinned and started into an energetic version of "Rockin' Robin." The hobos and some of the guests moved toward the fire, walking sticks in hand, to take up the dance. They circled the fire, everyone moving clockwise, two or three abreast, stepping in time to the music—young children and old timers alike. People were smiling, singing along, holding hands, and kicking their feet. Frog, a hobo who must get around in a motorized chair, guided his chair with one hand and danced with a young red-haired girl the hobos had "adopted" for the duration of the convention. When the song finished, all the dancers returned to their seats and the bride and groom moved back to the tree, where Black Knight waited.

"You must consider carefully the means by which you choose to settle disagreements, by selecting a method that neither offends nor hurts the other person," he cautioned the bride and groom. And he lifted the paper he held in his hands and began to read the vows:

"You are the way you are, and it's okay with me for you to be that way—Do you accept that vow?"

"Yes," the bride and groom answered separately, as they were expected to do for each of the remaining vows:

"May my love for you always be greater than my need for you—Do you accept that?"

"I will always do right, even if it's not what I want—Do you accept that?"

"I will help you be a success in your way—Do you accept that?"

After each vow, Black Knight waited for their answers. Then he asked one more question: "Do you have any hesitation or mental reservations whatsoever about accepting these vows?"

"No," Wingnut and Sunflower each said.

"This is a double-ring ceremony," Black Knight announced. On that cue, a musician began to play Mendelssohn's "Bridal March" on his recorder, showing the first bit of "tradition" recognized by the non-hobo spectators. "With this ring, I thee wed," they each said as they placed a ring on the other's finger.

"Ladies and Gentlemen of Britt," said Black Knight, "I give you Sunflower and Wingnut." He turned to Wingnut, "You may kiss the bride." The couple kissed as the crowd hooted, hollered, and applauded.

"May you be well, secure, peaceful, happy, and content—and live your life in gentle kindness," Black Knight said to them. He spoke again to the crowd. "As a hobo tradition, we have one more thing to do."

A hobo named Sunrise joined Black Knight at the microphone. Over her denim clothes, she wore a ceremonial purple stole draped around her neck and extending down to her knees. A white cross had been embroidered on each end. In her hands was a small jar of oil. As she applied it to the couple, Black Knight said to them: "We anoint you, we appoint you, we dub you, and we name you husband and wife throughout this lifetime."

He turned to the audience and asked, "Is she and he worthy?" The audience cheered its approval. "Yes, they're worthy!"

"You are officially hobo married," the Black Knight said. "Congratulations."

PART III – HOBO ROAD STORIES

"It takes a thousand voices to tell a single story."
—Native American saying

In the process of filming for our documentary, also titled Mulligan Stew, *we wanted firsthand accounts of the hobo life. We asked some of the hobos about their experiences on the road and let them tell their own stories, focusing on whatever they thought was important. In this section, you'll read stories about riding steam, hoboing during the Great Depression, being beat up and left for dead, riding to find work, and riding for the pure pleasure of travel.*

IOWA BLACKIE

Iowa Blackie, who was elected King in 1993–1994, caught the Westbound in 2011 and was buried in the hobo section of Evergreen Cemetery in Britt. His passing was often discussed by fellow hobos, and in that sense, he was part of the 2011 convention. In this book, others have told part of his story (see the remembrance in the "The Public Hobo Memorial Service" section, earlier in this book, and Minneapolis Jewel's recollections later in this section). Because we couldn't interview him directly, we've included several of Iowa Blackie's poems, which give a personal account of his life as a hobo. The selections included here are from The Absolute Latest Collected Works: Prose, Poetry and Stories of 'Iowa (Poet) Blackie.' *In that collection, he covered a gamut of topics—from memories of childhood and teachers, to observations about nature, his emotions, his Harley-Davison, his hobo friends, the deep loneliness he felt at times, and of course, freight yards and freight trains.*

THAT SHANTY BY THE MAIN

Not much this shanty by the main
Four cobbled walls with single door
Some boarded over window panes
A wooden bench and bare wood floor

Sufficient though in case of rain
A temporary place to kip
While waiting for an out bound train
An interlude on lengthy trips

God bless those men who built this shack
Providing me a place to sit
Or lie to rest my weary back
When I no longer can submit

MEMORIES

from *My First Train Ride and Other Poems*

Those memories of teenage years
Were bittersweet to say the least
But even after all those tears
The sweetness of them had not ceased

My rambling life began back then
The morning when I caught that train
Oh retrospective sweetness when
I climbed aboard to ease my pain

Imbued with feelings strange and new
While riding down that railroad track
Those early moments precious few
That wondrous rhythmic click and
    clack

The rumbling cadence slow at first
Began to quicken loud and strong
Instilling in me avid thirst
For wanderlusting railroad song

Before too long the early light
Evolved into the crack of dawn
Upon the spinning wheels a sight
To which my life would be drawn

Despite the shortness of that ride
The combination cast its spell
Straight life would soon be cast aside
In love with wanderlust I fell

More than mere riding on the train
Most aspects of the hobo life
Appealed to me despite the pain
Potential ever-present strife

The sleeping in an old boxcar
Or cooking out along the road
While roaming out there near and far
It would be likely with my load

A pair of overalls and shoes
With red bandanna and warm socks
Seemed just the clothing I should
    choose
To live the life and ride a box.

Since I could not leave home just yet
I lingered round the yards and dreamed
Of distant years when I would get
My freedom or that way it seemed

I'd have to bide my time and wait
For someday freedom would be mine
Escaping on a rumbling freight
And in the hobo jungles dine.

A Dreary Box Car Flop

It was a dreary painful night
When I approached that empty car
The shelter which to ease my plight
Inside I bore a heavy scar

I climbed in with my gear and then
Walked over to the northern wall
Where with my bag I once again
Felt very lonely and so small

I spread my roll upon the floor
And soon had crawled inside to rest
Such loneliness I felt before
Had surely put me to the test

I wondered at the hurt I felt
And why I had to feel that way
The feeling had within me dwelt
And let me far too long astray

The gentle patter of that rain
Should soothe a person feeling low
As would a slowly rocking train
I've been there so I ought to know

I turned my face unto the wall
Which was of wood and then I wept
It should not be that way at all
Amidst the pain at last I slept

CARDBOARD
(excerpt)

Though open boxcars on a train
I am about to ride are nice
More pleased am I should it contain
Clean cardboard sheets to be precise

Attractive in its simple way
A useful barrier to cold
The mattress where myself to lay
And if enough to thickness fold

I almost hate to leave a car
Where cardboard has been plentiful
Because so seldom ever are
The cardboards sheets so bountiful

GRANDPA

Grandpa is a bridger. Here he talks about what it was like to ride steam and why he rode. At the end of his interview, he sang a song about his travels. Grandpa was elected King in 2001–2002.

About Hobos and Riding Steam

The word hobo comes from two words: hoe boy. A person who carries his hoe was the first to get a job because there was no equipment, and a farmer couldn't afford to buy that many hoes. So he hired the hoe boys.

The basic hobo movement started after the civil war. There was no protection for those who joined the army, so when they came back they didn't have a job. So they went out looking for work.

A hobo is a person who is willing to work to cover his travels. A tramp travels but doesn't want to work.

One thing that's really noticeable when riding steam is that you get dirty. You're in the coal smoke—you really have no choice. So the hobos used to carry a bindle, which was some clean clothes… When you get to stop for a while, he would take a bath under a bridge or someplace where there's a stream, and he would change clothes and wear clean clothing.

Why Hop a Train?

Fun. I really had no reason to leave home. Council Bluffs, where I lived at the time, was the railroad center of that area, and all the trains would come into Council Bluffs in Omaha, across the Missouri River. I was interested in the hobos—I had already been here at Britt, and I understood the hobos and I related to them. So I rode the trains. They were short rides because I had no reason to go look for a job or leave home.

They accepted the fact that my rides were short when I ran for King of the Hobos in 2001 to 2002. When you are elected King, [first] you put your name on the board that you're going to run. Then you must go through a hobo screening where they will ask you questions and so forth until they understand that they want you for a King. Then we go down to the park and you give a speech in front of about 3,000 people and you win by applause. There's about 3 to 5 candidates. You win by applause and they have people around the crowd so they can judge the crowd.

Sidetracked

When my wife [M.A.D. Mary] was elected Queen, she wanted to ride. She had never ridden freight trains. So we had a fellow take us to Clinton, Iowa, and we went all the way across Illinois to Chicago, at night.

We got sidetracked, waiting for a train to come the other way, and I looked down the track and here comes a fellow with a flashlight. You don't use a flashlight around a train unless you're working for them, you know? So we got down and we heard him crunching along in the gravel there, and he went two cars beyond us and got up and he looked in the car. And then he got down and came back our way and went two cars the other way, behind us, and got up and looked in the car. And then he came back our way again, and the next thing we knew we were looking at a flashlight.

It was a college student. He said, "Are you riding, too?" [Grandpa laughs] He wasn't working for the railroad, he was just inexperienced. It was his first ride, and we thought we'd been caught. The chances are that all they'd do is put you off the train. Then they unhooked us at west Chicago—we were planning on going into Proviso yard—at 2 in the morning. It was a double-stack we were riding, and we stayed there until it got light. The fellow that unhooked us climbed over the car we were in about 10 feet away from us. I just figured he saw us and let it go. Most of the railroad people are pro hobo, but [not] the railroad cops. The reason they get you off the trains is because of insurance. If they had a wreck, they could be sued.

"I have a song," Grandpa announced, and he began singing these words:

Grandpa's Song: "The Train Ride to Nowhere"

In the summer of '96 in Baldwin City town.
The railroad had a festival; the hobos gathered 'round
The townfolk bought their tickets though the rain was coming down
The ticket man was selling rides to Nowhere

Well Nowhere was a place found at the far end of the line
The only way you'd know it is a little railroad sign
The passengers had boarded, you could hear that whistle whine
That day the train was bound for Nowhere

The train left Baldwin City
It was chugging down the line
Heading out to nowhere, everyone was feeling fine
It never got to Nowhere 'cuz the freight guy jumped the line
We were derailed on the train ride to nowhere

A very special lady was riding on that train
She always helped the hoboes, and Derail was her name
She got initiated and she earned a little fame
When we derailed on the train ride to Nowhere

Texas madman rode a tank car in the platform on the top
When the car before him jumped the rail, began to reel and rock
He waved his arms and shouted, trying to get the train to stop
When we derailed on the train ride to Nowhere
We derailed on the train ride to Nowhere

"Now that is 100 percent true—every part of it," he said. "Derail became Queen the year I was King."

LONG LOST LEE

Long Lost Lee rode during the Great Depression, right after graduating from high school. Here he talks about the Great Depression and what he learned as he traveled through Yellowstone, met up with bulls, knocked at back doors, and experienced the kindness of strangers. He has never run for King.

Run-ins with Bulls—and Other Dangers

When I started riding the rails, it was back in '37, and that was just about the middle of the Depression. That was the year I graduated from high school, and there were no jobs and there was no money. I had a buddy who was in the same predicament, and he said maybe we can get a job in Chicago. So I said "Let's go." We had a friend in Chicago, and maybe he could help us out.

We hopped the Green Bay and Western and then transferred to the other rail that took us into Chicago. We met our buddy and had him checking out jobs for us, but there were no jobs, so we thought, "Well, let's head back West. We could maybe get some jobs back West."

As it was, we were in the train station, and the passenger train, the Limited from Chicago to Minneapolis, was about ready to take off. My buddy and I climbed up in the coal car — in the passenger trains, there was no place to ride as far as the cars were concerned — we went into the coal car that was behind the engine. There was a place that prevented the coal from getting back any farther. The coal was in the front half of the coal car, and the second half was for the water. So we started out and nobody knew we were up there. As we went along a little ways further, the engineer decided, "Hey, I don't want those guys behind there." So he had a steam hose and he'd climb up on the ol' coal bin and steam over us, and we'd have to climb back under that shelf that would protect us. We did ride into Minneapolis and we got off as if we were paid riders and thought we were pretty smart.

The bulls we bumped into quite often, and I heard them shoot their guns. But I still feel that they really didn't hate us guys as much as we thought that they did, and even if we heard gunshots, I'm sure it was up in the air. Of course, we were faster runners than they were, and I never was caught by a railroad bull.

* * *

We were into this town that had a warehouse. I think it was a cotton warehouse. A lot of blacks were in the warehouse. We spent the night there, and the next morning the cops came in and said, "Okay boys, out of town. We're not going to put you over in the railroad tracks because we want you to really get out of town." So down the road we went, probably 20 of us, walking to the next town. Probably 20 miles or so.

Along the way we thumbed this one car that picked us up, and away we went. It was a pickup truck, and after we went down the road a ways, I made small talk and asked the driver, "Aren't you afraid to pick up strangers like us?"

"Naw," he says, "I like to help you guys out. I was never afraid of you. If you had said the wrong thing or done the wrong thing…" And he pulled this revolver out—he had it down in the corner of the seat. " I had no problem with you boys. "You were good boys." Then he took us into the next town and we went on our way in a boxcar.

Learning the Rules of the Road

When I first started out, this one hobo sort of took me under his wing; he thought maybe I was a good guy. He told me his story. He was the engineer of the Elevated in Chicago. And it was a good job. He said he was a drinker. He became an alcoholic, and he had a wreck with the El and he lost his job. He had a house, but he was still drinking. He started selling things out of the house…

At that time I was about 19 years old and pretty green about the rules of the road. We would pull into a town, and the first thing he would do is go over to the tavern. In those days they had spittoons in the taverns, and he would ask if he could clean the spittoons and do any kind of work for a drink, because he was an alcoholic.

But he also told us that you want to knock on the right kind of doors for your food. You want to knock only on the blue-collar house doors because they're the kind of people that will give you a bite to eat. He said if you knock on the doors of those big fancy houses, chances are you're not going to be fed.

Adventures in Yellowstone Park

From [Minneapolis] we went over to the railroad yards and hopped a boxcar and we went west. We got as far as Cody, Wyoming, near the Yellowstone Park. We got off the boxcar and said, "Let's go to Yellowstone Park." We didn't have any money or anything.

We tried to hitch a ride from Cody, and we got a ride with a bread truck. It was heading into the park to do business. He said, "Yeah, boys, I'll take you into the park." When we got to the park we asked if he had any day-old bread and any other things, and he had a sack and he filled the sack up with odds and ends he collected as he made his delivery there. We left him and walked through the park a ways.

That night we had no place to go but out into the woods. We found a place under a tree and in the middle of the night, we felt a few sounds around us, and finally there were a lot of sounds around us. The bears smelled the sweet rolls and whatever we had in the sack. We held our breath for the rest of the night and never moved. We were scared shitless. They were circling, but I guess they were good bears because they didn't attack. We did make it to morning and got out onto the road and hitched a ride.

A young married couple picked us up and they had a rumble seat. We sat in the rumble seat and made the tour of Yellowstone Park like we might have owned it. As we left the park, a Catholic priest picked us up and took us over to the community a few miles on where he was going to do the last rites on some firefighters who had been fighting the forest fire. I could see the smoke off in the distance. When he was through with that he took us back into Cody, and we hopped a train and we went on our way.

The Sheriff and Bull Durham

We were on a flatcar going down through Chicago, south through Illinois, and we thought maybe we could get a job on a boat. Where those boats would be going, I have no idea, but that was in our minds until we got down to southern Illinois and word came out: "Gosh, you boys better not go any further south because they're picking them up and putting the hobos into the county farms." It was time to gather the vegetables, or whatever the county farms grow, and they said, 'They'll work you there, and there's no pay.'

So then we decided we'd head west. I remember we got into Nebraska or Oklahoma... We stopped at this little town and we'd already knocked on a few doors and we'd had plenty to eat. We were walking down the main street and this fella on the corner was rolling a cigarette from a Bull Durham sack, and I bummed a Bull Durham off of him. "Sure," he said. "Roll your own." I made my cigarette and I thanked him and we went on.

In the evening, there was a culvert on the edge of town and my buddy and I thought that would be a good place to spend the night, out of the way, but about dusk, somebody up on the bank said, 'Come on boys, we're going to take you in.' They took us into the jail and we overnighted there. Next morning, low and behold, they brought us a little bite to eat. As we were leaving the jail, I looked over into the office and here was this fellow that I bummed the cigarette makings from...he was the sheriff. We were about to leave and he says "Here." And he threw us a bag of Bull Durham and said, "Have a good trip, boys."

Lessons from the Road

Most of the hobos were just young kids in the same predicament that we were. I can remember riding the freights on top, and there would be a hundred, two hundred of us...

We were in Kansas City and we were under a bridge. There were a half a dozen of us young hobos. We were under the bridge and we decided we would all go out and bum our food, and bring back what we could and then we would divide it up. That way we'd get a good variety. I went my way and hit one house and they said "Sure, come on in and clean up the table," which I did. When I got through cleaning up the table, I was full. Then I went on and got some other food items at a few other houses and then went back under the bridge that evening. The other guys came back, and they all had this and that, and we divided up our food, and we each got a portion. I took my part of the food as well, which was substantial again, and I ate that. But not having eaten for a day or two, I was hungry when I ate from the table the first time, and then I gorged myself with the second helping.

Oh, God, I got sick...I ate too much! My system just couldn't handle all that food. So I was sick and threw up all that night, and the next day I was sick, and I threw up again. That was a story about humans when they get greedy, you know? That happens today in the stock market, and people get greedy. And it happens with greedy people. You get sick! [Long Lost Lee laughs.] That was a good experience.

Farmwork

If you could get any work at all, like farmwork, they'd take you in and feed you and maybe at the end of the month they might give you four dollars or five dollars. There just was no money.

The Kindness of Strangers

In all of my three years of riding the rails, I knocked on doors of blue-collar houses, and I don't think I was ever denied something to eat. If it wasn't, 'I'll fix you up with something,' it was, 'Come on in and clean up the table.' I learned then that it was blue collar people who had concern for their fellow mankind, and in towns and cities, the old communities where people know each other, the same thing holds true. If somebody needs a little help, even today, they're there to give you a hand—if not to feed you, to raise some money to send you for this or that. There's a certain class of people that are forever looking out for their brothers.

UNCLE FREDDIE

Uncle Freddie is a bridger. Here he tells about his life as a hobo, his friendship with Road Hog, and his run-ins with bulls. He was elected King in 2011–2012.

Comparing Then and Now

How was it in the old days? Well, the tracks every 30 feet had [a join] and that's where you got that clickety clack. Now the tracks are welded, so you don't get that clickety clack.

The floors in the boxcar were wood; they absorbed the sound. Now they're all steel. They used to have cabooses, now they have the red box at the back and it's called FRED—the Freight Rear-End Detector. It was named after me. [He laughs.]

The Lure of Hoboing

It's being free. You sleep when you want to sleep. You eat when you want to eat. You work when you want to work. I had a ton of jobs. When I applied for Social Security, a young kid, maybe 17 or 18 years old, I don't know how old he was, he punched it up on the computer and said, "My Lord, I've never seen anything like this." Then he flipped it over and there's another page, and another page. He said, "I've never seen a person have this many jobs!"

I said, "Well, I was a traveling man. I was in construction." I did everything… I pearl dive, which is washing dishes, I've been on three cattle drives, I broke horses, I hoed watermelon. I did all kind of jobs. Dug irrigation ditches. I *worked*. I worked hard.

So I've done everything I wanted to in life, and this year I'm running for King. I could possibly make it. I love Britt. And I do want to thank all the servicemen and women that are giving us that right to be here. To celebrate.

I rode across the United States several times. All over the United States. And I call the United States my home. But I reside in Minnesota now.

I hit the rails for the first time at 14 years old. Then, after the service I hit the rails for maybe eight years. I settled down, and then started riding again in the '70s up until about six or seven years ago. My last ride was from Marquette, Iowa, to St. Paul.

On Friendship

I've met so many people. At Christmastime, I get cards from all over the United States. But a lot of [my friends] are dead now. In the last five years, I lost probably 10 of the people I rode with. I never rode with Steam Train, but I was very close to him as far as knowledge goes. He was a very smart man as far as being a hobo. So many of the guys I have much respect for because they do what they want to do, you know.

Being honest is the main thing. Being honest with yourself and your friends. I got friends all over the United States.

About Road Hog

Road Hog came and lived with me in California for a month. We traveled together, rode together for a while. I was up at Dunsmuir four times—that's where he resided. He took care of the cemetery up there. He told me one time, "Uncle Freddie," he says, "I need a couple of dollars to get a roll of paper towels and a bottle of Windex and by 5 o'clock tonight I'll have enough money for a motel and full-course dinner." And by God he did.

The buckle on his gravestone, you see on his tombstone—he give me that probably twenty years ago. Beautiful buckle. I never wore it because it was so beautiful. But then I gave it to Tuck when he became King. He probably had it for 10 years. And now Tuck made the tombstone for him and he embedded it in the tombstone. It made its full rounds.

[*Tuck, who was sitting beside Uncle Freddie, said, "I didn't know it."*]

That was Road Hog's buckle in the first place. I traveled a lot with Road Hog. He was a very smart man, as far as education goes for riding the rails. He was the boss.

Bulls and Other Dangers

In Sparks, Nevada, I can remember a policeman, not a railroad bull, and he said "You get on that train"—and it was boogying—"or you go to jail. Either way." [*Freddie got on the train, he said.*]

There were a lot of scary times. Of course, my mouth got me in trouble a few times. They picked me up in Reading, California, Shasta County, and I remembered very well, that they could only hold me 72 hours, for investigation. So when my 72 hours were up, I start rattlin' my tin cup and they came and said, "What you want?" And I said "My 72 hours are up, and I know it's the law that you have to turn me loose or book me on something."

They said, "Okay, you do know the law."

So they give me my gear back and I walked down the steps to the side-walk and two cops got me and put me back in there for *another* 72 hours. [Freddie laughs.] So I know to keep quiet if you don't know what you're talking about.

M.A.D. MARY

M.A.D. Mary was elected Queen in 2000–2001. She is married to the hobo named Grandpa. Here she talks about her first and only ride.

Catching Out

I was Queen of the Hobos in 2000 to 2001. I've actually ridden only once, and that was the year I was Queen. We hopped a freight in Clinton, Iowa, and rode to west Chicago. In west Chicago we were sidetracked, so we couldn't go any farther. In the process, we thought we'd almost been caught. We got to Chicago and thought we got caught again, but we weren't caught then either. We stayed in the double-stack car until morning, and when we started walking out, this long coal train was coming out of the yard, going toward Wisconsin, and [the engineer] actually stopped the train so we could cross the tracks before he went out—so we wouldn't have to wait for that long train to go by.

I'd love to do it again. I was ready to go again right away, but in this day and age it's dangerous to ride, so we haven't done it again.

A bridger is someone who rode steam trains, and then when diesels came around, they rode diesel trains. My husband is a bridger. He rode steam trains back in the thirties and forties, and when we went on our ride when I was Queen, he rode the [diesel] train, so that makes him a bridger.

LUTHER THE JET

Luther the Jet was elected King in 1995-1996. He often sings a capella at hobo gatherings, adding his voice to the ceremonies honoring those who have caught the Westbound and making up political verses to the tune of old labor songs. In this story Luther describes the pleasures and trials of a ride he took in 1995. (Previously published in a zine titled Something About a Train, *"Night Trains" is included here by permission of the author.)*

Night Trains

"Take the Illinois Central!" the great and wise Train Doc Norton said to me. "They've laid off almost all their cops, and the yard here in Chicago is a breeze." I was on my way from Madison, Wisconsin, to Amory, Mississippi, for the annual Railroad Days Festival, and Train Doc's prescription sounded like just the ticket—or I mean just the free ride! Without further ado I took the city transit and bus line down to Homewood, on the far south side, and started to sniff around Markham Yard. It was a breeze all right—compact, secluded, unlighted, with no cops in sight—but unfortunately the night freight for Memphis had just blown out of town, and the switchman advised me there wouldn't be another one till the next morning. I found a line of derelict cabooses tucked away behind the rip track and bedded down comfortably for the night.

The next morning was Easter Sunday, as glorious a day as God ever made. Through the murky windows of the caboose I spotted some big road power backing into the yard and hightailed it over to the departure tracks just in time to find the leeward porch of a grainer about midway back in train CHFE, the daily run to Fulton, Kentucky. We were out of town in a trice, sailing along through the pleasant suburban countryside south of Chicago.

Children and grownups were outside in their Easter finery, the adults looking stiff and uncomfortable and the kids rolling eggs, desecrating Easter baskets, and otherwise having a good time. Lilacs and redbud were in bloom—a combination that for me translates into an instant high. I hung off the porch of the grainer, breathing in the warm spring air and waving like a fool to passing motorists.

All went swimmingly for the first 150 miles or so, until we neared the depot at Mattoon, Illinois. I knew there was a small yard south of town but I figured everything would be deserted on Easter Sunday. Wrong! As we rolled slowly by the station I spotted a white car that looked suspiciously like a police vehicle. I saw a guy standing in the doorway wearing gray trousers, white shirt, and black tie. In the next instant this guy spotted me. He tore out of the station, jumped in his car and started to follow the slowing train. His route wasn't directly beside the tracks, but took him out of sight along some city streets. I saw him tear out of the depot parking lot and turn a corner, but I knew he would soon reappear.

We stopped a mile or so south of town. There was now a gravel road on both sides of the train. I looked back along one side and then the other, ready to make a quick jump in order to avoid the impending collar. But the white car never showed up, even though we switched at Mattoon for better than half an hour. Can you believe it? I now figured this guy would pick me off at some crossing south of town, so I was extra vigilant as we pulled out. But in spite of working up a sweat over all the possibilities, I never saw him again.

It wasn't until we stopped to switch the yard at Effingham, in late afternoon, that I found out what was going on. The conductor walked the train to check a big cut on the next track, and as he passed my grainer I hailed him:

"You gonna set me off here?"

"No, I'm not. But you almost got set off at Mattoon—do you know that?

"Well, I saw that cop jump in his car."

"That wasn't a cop. It was the yard clerk. He was scared to come after you so he called *me*. I said it's not my job to bounce people off trains, so I'm not going to. They said they're gonna turn me in. I said go ahead. As far as I'm concerned you can stay on."

"Thanks for the favor!"

"Where you headed?"

"Memphis."

"This car you're on should be going straight through. Just stay out of sight, and don't get hurt."

"Thanks again."

So there it was, my own private sleeper to Memphis. Out of Effingham we ran into a couple heavy thunderstorms, but as soon as things dried off a little I laid out my bedroll, dozing off as the sun set over the prairies. We turned off the IC passenger main at Edgewood about 15 miles south of Effingham, then stopped out in the woods near Bluford for a crew change. In the gathering dark I could see the ghostly white forms of dogwoods in the neighboring forests. Believe it or not, this line goes through three tunnels, each more than 2,000 feet long, as it descends from the plains to the banks of the Ohio. I got up momentarily to look at the big Ohio River bridge near Paducah, then slept right through Fulton and whatever work we did there.

The dawn of Easter Monday found us just a few miles out of Memphis. I hung on till we pulled into the north end of Johnston Yard, about three miles southeast of downtown, then hopped off and washed up at the switch shanty. The switchmen, as friendly here as in Chicago, said there would be a transfer run to the BN yard sometime during the day, but they didn't know when. It turned out the BN man didn't show up till around noon, and didn't get back out of the IC yard till around 3:00 p.m. But I had made contact with the BN conductor and so was assured of a nice ride on a grainer. We made our way uptown to Yale Junction, near the twin Mississippi River bridges, then turned east for the 15-mile run to the BN yard at Capelville. It was almost dark by the time we pulled in, so I had supper at the Subway on Capelville Road and bedded down in an empty semi in the piggyback yard, well away from the hordes of mosquitoes down in the weeds.

Capelville isn't the size of North Platte or Proviso, but it's still a big yard and can get a little confusing. I didn't find an eastbound till about 4 o'clock the next afternoon, and even though the conductor specifically told me they weren't making a stop at Amory, I climbed aboard a dirty gondola, the only ride on the train. This is something that might charitably be termed a miscalculation. I put a bandana over my nose and mouth, but still looked like a coal miner when I was unceremoniously booted off the train. An overzealous section foreman spotted me when we went into emergency right in front of his project near Blue Springs, Mississippi, about 75 miles out. I had to hoof it into beautiful downtown Blue Springs and hitch a ride to Tupelo, about ten miles east. The next day I caught another ride to Amory, where by noon I was sitting in the dining room of the old Park Hotel, enjoying a light lunch of corn muffins and orange juice and chatting amiably with the Texas Madman.

The Festival at Amory was well organized, as always, and the folks there as hospitable as anyplace on earth. Festival factotum Dickie Miller took us around to sing and give programs at two of the local schools, plus the nursing home where the hobos have always been welcome. Buddy Carlisle and his uncle James, past and present stalwarts of the shortline Mississippian Railway, made us feel right at home. And Glo Buie, proprietress of the Nibble Nook Cafe, had us all over for one of her incredible breakfasts, the dishes all homemade and the tables groaning with plenty.

I had arranged to meet up with Dave Murphy, a young rider from Dallas, in order to take a little jaunt with him in the direction of the Ozarks. As the week drew to a close I got worried that Dave might not show up, but on Friday evening I suddenly found him sitting right next to me at the campfire, just in on a freight and ready to catch out again the next day.

All right! We got a great ride out of Amory, by means best left vague, and by nightfall on Saturday found ourselves back at the big yard in Capelville. Here confusion reigned, and just to make things worse there was a light rain coming on. We let a couple westbounds slip away from us in the dark before we spotted the blinking Freddie of a westbound piggyback some distance down the track. Don't you know this guy started moving, just enough to torment us, before we could even get close. Tempted beyond endurance, Dave broke into a run, while I trotted along as fast as I could. The train stopped just long enough for us to catch up; Dave took the second car ahead and I got on the very last one, crouching under the big tires of a trailer while the rains descended.

What a catch! An open piggyback in the rain. Dave decided to unroll his bundle and lie down in a little dry spot in the center of his car; I stayed huddled behind my tires and managed to keep fairly dry, if a little cramped. Lucky for us, the rain was warm and not too heavy. In cooler conditions we might have had serious problems with hypothermia.

This was not a pleasant ride. We hung on all the way to Thayer, the next division point, bouncing along in the misty gloom. When we finally got off it was nearly 4:00 a.m. I knew there was an old caboose right next to the depot and local police station, so that's where we headed, getting ourselves situated very quietly so we could go to sleep about twenty feet away from the local constable. He never bothered us. It turned out there was only one bunk left in the old crummy, and Dave, gentleman that he is, gave it to me. I was in sore need of a soft place to stretch out; no sooner had I laid down than my legs started to cramp, an effect of the chill and the long confinement in one position. I piled everything that was dry on top of me and finally got warmed up enough to relax and go to sleep.

Thayer, beautiful Thayer! This little burg in the Ozarks was named, as was Amory, for one of the Boston capitalists who financed the old Kansas City, Memphis, and Birmingham, later the Frisco, and now part of the BNSF. It's one of the nicest railroad division points in the land, a balm for weary travelers who are tired of big cities and giant yards. When I woke up, the birds were singing and there was still a misty haze in the air. It was 10:30 a.m. Dave was sitting on the floor beside me, quietly reading a book.

"Boy, you really slept!" he said.

I thanked him for letting me saw wood as long as I wanted. And I really felt rested, too. We made our way over to the main road, and the only operational restaurant in town. Sitting down to a huge breakfast, we were greeted by a young guy at the table next to us:

"You boys travellin' through?"

"Yes," we replied, somewhat in hesitation as we weren't sure of his reasons for asking.

"Well, I'm the engineer on the next westbound, a fast doublestack. We're due out about 12:30. Why don't you catch the third or fourth unit and ride over to Springfield with us?"

How about that? We walked back over to the yard and lay low in some weeds near the depot till the westbound pulled in, then quick as lighting we got inside the fourth unit. As soon as we left town we turned on the heat and got all our damp clothes and packs spread out inside the cab. It must have looked like Monday's wash, to anybody who was looking, but we hardly saw a soul over the beautiful rolling country of southern Missouri. Dave got off this train at Springfield, to return to Dallas, but I stayed on clear to Kansas City, and the next day caught the Santa Fe back to Chicago. So the trip to Amory was all in all a great success, in spite of having included a couple rides I wouldn't want to try again.

FROG

Frog was elected King in 1997–1998. Here he talks about his first ride, his friendship with Road Hog USA, and about being beaten and left by the tracks.

Friendship—and the Hobo Hustle with Road Hog USA

[Frog began by talking about Road Hog USA]

Our friendship actually began in 1988 when I ran into him. I, like Luther the Jet, ran into him at the cemetery that he was caretaker for. He actually lived in the caretaker's shack and it was a rumble-down old shack along the Southern Pacific Railway track line. I don't remember the exact mile marker, but it was right there in Dunsmuir. It was a beautiful, beautiful spot. I woke up in the cemetery and he invited me in for coffee, and I had coffee with him, and then he says, "It's just about beer-thirty time, isn't it?"

So I had a beer with him and he said, "Let's go do the hobo hustle." We went downtown Dunsmuir. He had squeegees and a water bucket, just an empty water bucket, and a couple bottles of Windex, and some newspapers we picked up in the free boxes, the advertisement for real estate and what not. To us it was just window-wiping material, and we went down along the main street of Dunsmuir. I believe it was about 30 different shops along downtown Dunsmuir, and by the end of our day—and our day really only lasted three and a half or four hours, because I was on one side of the street and Road Hog was on the other side of the street—by the end of our 4-hour work day, we had made probably about $100 apiece, or maybe more, and we went and sat in the bar and had one beer…it was the local bar for the people of Dunsmuir… it seemed like all the people 60 and younger went to that bar, so I walked in there, and lo and behold, Hobo Spike was in there with his girlfriend at the time—she's now his wife—and we shot the breeze for a few minutes.

He thought I'd come a distance to see Road Hog, when basically, I'd just gotten there on my way somewheres else. I didn't care where I was going....It was late spring, past June, and I was heading to Montana where I could just jungle out for two, three weeks at a time and camp out along the Kootenay River. I used to enjoy going to the town of Libby, Montana, and just camp there for weeks on end. It wasn't just myself. I had a partner at the time, but he just hadn't caught up with me yet from our last stop, which had been Roseville. But he got work, and he worked much later than I wanted him to be out and working. We never know when we're going to get a job, and you take what you can get when you need money.

After that 1988 experience, I didn't see Road Hog again until August of 1995, when I came here for my first hobo convention, and he was here. And I said, "My God, I remember you. What's your name again?" He said, "You should remember my name, I have an easy name to remember— Road Hog. Don't you know what a road hog is?

'Cause Road Hog had ridden steam. I had never ridden steam because I didn't start riding freight trains until I was 20 years old back in 1970.

Catching Out—The First Ride

I had to get out of Jacksonville, Florida. I got thrown off the beaches. The judge gave me 24 hours to get out of town. "Get your butt out of my town and don't come back. We're not going to have you transients along our wonderful waterfronts and destroying our property and littering our property. It belongs to the city and as a member of this community and we're asking you to leave, and you have exactly 24 hours. If I see you again before me in this court tomorrow morning, you're going to do 30 days. "

It really prompted me—I'd already spent the night in the jail there for trespassing. It was no big thing. I got up and started trying to hitch-hike. I walked perhaps 15, 16 miles. Not a soul stopped to pick me up. That was along Interstate 10. Back then, back in the early 70s, the highway patrol weren't giving tickets for trespassing like they do today. At the end of my walk, I ran into a black man. He was just sitting across the street from where I was hitchhiking, and he yells at me, "Why don't you just catch out?" I was scratching my head wondering, *What the hell is he talking about? Catch out? I'm trying to hitchhike out.* So I said, "What do you mean?"

He said, "You never rode a train before? Come on, I'll show you how to get out of town. It might take us a few hours. Just sit here with me. I'll buy you a beer."

I wasn't even of age to have a beer, but my eyes popped open…A beer… I'll figure out what he's trying to do here. He runs across the way to where I was at and he helps me carry my stuff across the highway. He says, "You're even packing like a tramp or a 'bo. Don't you ride trains?"

I said, "Never have."

He says, "Don't you want to get out of town?"

I says, "Yes sir, I do."

He says, "Well you're not going to do it standing on that highway, because there isn't a soul in this town that will give you a ride out of here. Look at you, you're dirty, filthy. You look like you spent the night in jail. Didn't they give you a shower?"

They just took me out of my cell and brought me to the courtroom. That morning I went before the judge and the judge threw me out of town. So I'm telling him all this and he says, "I'll show you what to do. It's a one-time deal. Don't go expecting this everytime you hit a town. But I'll get you out of here."

I said, "But where is it going to take me?"

He said, "Does it matter to you? You're going on a freight train ride. You'll like it and you get to where we're going to stop at, just get up and go. You'll be out of Jacksonville. You're not going to spend the 30 days in jail."

I said okay. It was about 4:30 in the afternoon when I ran into him, and it was getting about 9:30, 10 o'clock. It's getting mighty dark out here. I don't know if a train is going to stop here. There'd been several trains that went by us, but they kept on going.

He said, "Your train will come in when it comes in. When it gets here you just get on."

Lo and behold, about eleven o'clock that night, here comes a train. It stops right smack in front of us, and there's all kinds…boxcars, grain cars, gondolas, and I've got no idea what one car or the other was called. I know that now…I actually rode for 31 years from that day on. My first ride was a ride that intrigued me so much. I fell in love with the rails. I continued to ride for 31 years.

Left for Dead

In 1995 I had been beaten by a gang of kids while I was waiting on a train. Beaten and robbed—and they actually left me for dead alongside the railroad tracks in North Dakota. That day, the only thing I remember was being bashed in the back of the head three times. At the end of the bash in the head, I came to—I was dead to the world. I could see the bone sticking out of my pant leg, and then realized all my belongings were gone. I eventually inched my way along two railroad tracks because there was no access road to that area where I'd been beaten. I was hidden in the bushes. I made my way to the tracks and I was flagging everyone and everything that's going by me. It was just trains. Finally, a track inspector came by me and I didn't know who or what he was or what he was doing. I didn't know if he was a railroad bull or a track inspector. They were trying to signal me away from the tracks, and I'm pointing down at my leg. And finally the driver is looking down at me and he said, "Get the hell away from the tracks. We'll get you some help."

Upon returning to the tracks, he brought an ambulance crew and a police officer. It was a small town. That police officer then called for the sheriff's department and two sheriffs came after that. I was loaded onto a gurney and onto an ambulance and brought to a hospital. The closest hospital—Fargo—was 30 miles away. They knew I would need surgery of some sort. The bone was sticking directly out of my pant leg. At the time, I had no idea they had stabbed me in the back 5 times as well. I survived it. I thought that the blood I was seeing on the back of my t-shirt was blood from the gash on the back of my head. I still have a nice 50-cent piece somewhere on the back of my head on my scalp. When my hair is short you can see it.

In 2001 the leg had degenerated to the point where I really couldn't walk anymore and carry my gear and catch a train safely without the help of someone else. I made my decision to retire at a hobo gathering in North Dakota. At that time I had achieved a lot and had reached a lot of my goals as a hobo and from my childhood days. I guess I was 51 when I actually got off the rails and retired.

When the sheriff's department was doing the investigation, they came to the conclusion—that they gave to the general public—that it was a transient situation, a transient crime that happened. Of course they were never able to find [the kids who did it]. Because I had laid for approximately 12 hours along the railroad tracks without help, they figured the 12 hours gave these five kids the opportunity to bundle up and get the hell out of town. However, I told the police after their third day of investigation that this interview is totally out of whack and you're trying to blame someone for doing something when I know for a fact they were well-dressed teenage boys with baseball bats and mitts and gloves—the whole works of a baseball player just coming from a ballgame. And I thought they were taking a shortcut home and they were hiding in the bushes. Obviously the kids had seen me from an adequate distance, and they made their way directly around me to the back side of me and they came up on me and one of them cracked me in the back of the head, and that's all I remember—my head flipping around and I'm looking at these five kids. To this day I can't imagine what they look like because I can't picture them in my mind anymore.

MINNEAPOLIS JEWEL

Jewel has been elected Queen four times: 1986–1987, 1991–1992, 1997–1998, and 2011–2012. Here she talks about her relationship and dealings with Iowa Blackie, her travels with him, and Blackie's obsession with her.

First Meeting at Hobo Days

I first met Iowa Blackie when I came to Britt in 1980. I came into the hobo jungle…and there were very few women there…and mostly it seemed like older men with white beards and one young man, who turned out to be Iowa Blackie. So we kind of glommed onto each other, although he had been here before, many times, and knew what was what. I was definitely the new kid on the block, so Iowa Blackie took me under his wing. He had ridden a few freight trains already at this time and was familiar with the hobo life. I know that a lot of the old-time hobos did not like having women in the jungle. Kind of like having women onboard a ship; they didn't really care for that.

So Blackie was kind of protective, and I stayed in the background. I didn't really say too much, I was more of an observer. So after Hobo Days ended, Blackie said, 'Oh, if I come up to Minneapolis, can I stay at your place for a day or two?' I said, 'Well, yes. Probably.' I only had a one-bedroom apartment with my daughter, who was 10 at the time, and I worked full-time as a means of support, and it was just her and I.

I told my daughter that this hobo was coming. She was rather taken aback. Blackie wore bib overalls, no shirt, no shoes…. He had kind of a scraggly beard and hair. I don't know what she thought, but she was used to me with strangers and stray animals, so she pretty much said, 'Oh, what the heck? Okay.'

Since I only had a 1-bedroom place, I told Blackie, 'You can sleep on the living room floor.' Which he did. And a couple days, of course, turned out to be a couple weeks. Finally, I told Blackie, 'You have to go because my daughter has school and I work my regular job.' I was a cook in downtown Minneapolis, and I had to go to work every day. So Blackie ended up exiting, and he stayed at a friend's house, and he said 'Can I still be in touch with you?' And I said 'Yes. We can be friends.'

So that started the course of 32 years of me and Iowa Blackie. I let him know in the very beginning that this was a friendship, a platonic friendship, and Blackie, being as smart as he was, knew the meaning of platonic, although he didn't want to heed that…He wanted a relationship, and I didn't want to be his wife or his lover or marry him, and that's what he wanted.

Blackie's Obsession with Jewel Begins

I moved from there to another apartment, and he followed me home. At this point he had gotten a truck and he was starting to do recycling. This was before recycling and scrapping became a popular thing. I know he followed me home one day in his recycling truck. And then I started receiving letters, at least once a day from Blackie, and I tried returning them [marked] Return to Sender, but he persisted, and he knew where I worked downtown as a cook, and he'd come into the building and he even asked my boss if he could have a job, even though he had no shirt, no shoes, once again. He was able to get a job as a phone book delivery person in that building. He was very tricky and very smart. So he delivered phone books for at least a month there so he could be by me and see me.

Jewel's First Ride

In 1991 I agreed with Blackie that I would take a ride with him. He and I left Minneapolis… he continuously took trains from Iowa to Minnesota. Back and forth. He had traveled other places, but this was his mainstay. So he knew the routes, the times the trains were leaving, approximately. He knew the yard workers; they knew him.

When we got down to the train station, he goes, 'Come on in this building because I know the people there and they'll let us stay in here.' And normally, that does not happen because you just don't go on railroad property unless you work for the railroad. But he seemed to feel that it was okay, that he knew these people and they knew him. So we went and waited in one of the work rooms, and we couldn't get a train out of there. So we had this other person take us to the Pig's Eye Yards in St. Paul…to catch a train. The train that came in had an old wooden boxcar, so I was quite impressed with that because you don't see the old wooden boxcars around anymore…

We were going to go down to Clinton, Iowa, to visit a friend named East Coast Charlie. East Coast Charlie worked in Clinton… at a shelter and a mission there. He worked in a thrift store they had. So I was very excited because I liked East Coast Charlie. He was an older guy, he was from the old school, and he had ridden quite a bit. I told Charlie, 'Yes, me and Blackie would be down to visit you.'

We got down to Clinton and the train slowed down. Clinton, Iowa, is where Mr. Peanut is from. They had a big, huge statue on top of a building—you could see off in the distance—of Mr. Peanut. The train slowed and slowed, and I kept saying to Blackie, 'Do we get off here? Do we get off here?' He wouldn't answer me, and it was making me mad because the train had slowed enough where I could have jumped off quite easily.

But I didn't know that Blackie was up to his devious methods, and he did not want me to go see East Coast Charlie. He wanted me to himself. So I didn't get off there—not knowing where to get off—and by the time I figured out what Blackie was up to, the train had started speeding up and we continued onward. It was too late to get off, and I was so mad because I knew he had sabotaged me getting off so he could have me to himself in the boxcar.

By this time it was about 5 in the evening. I had told Charlie we should be there pretty soon. Well, that didn't happen. The train continued on and picked up speed and at that point it was just too late to try and jump off. I was really ticked off at Blackie and said, 'Why didn't you tell me to get off where we could have gotten off?' I could see the mission was over here, not too far. Blackie had nothing to say, just kind of shrugged his shoulders and wouldn't answer me. The train kept going. I think we finally ended up down by the quad cities, where the train actually stopped and we got off.

At that point we had to do a turnaround to get back to Clinton, Iowa. I was really ticked off at Blackie because it upset the whole plan, plus, I only had a certain amount of time off from work. Where I worked in the restaurant, we did not have paid vacation; we did not have sick days; we did not have holidays. So any time I took off from work was a non-paid day for me. And I only had a certain amount of time I could be away from the restaurant.

So this put us back a couple of days and in a time crunch…We turned around, and this time we got off where we were supposed to get off. It was late at night, I think about 11 or 11:30, and it was pitch-pouring rain.

At the Mission

We got off the train and we proceeded to go to the mission to see if East Coast Charlie was still there. Blackie said, 'Oh…wait out here.' I waited in the rain and he came out of some building and said, 'Okay, we're going to go in here and sleep for the night. East Coast Charlie is not around.'

We went into the back door of this building and there was a couch there.…I took off my boots and just laid there, and it was dark and I couldn't see what was going on, but I was so tired I didn't care… the next morning I woke up and I looked around, and lo and behold, there were no women in there. It was all men. And they were all staring at me incredulously. They looked at me and said, 'Lady, what are you doing in here?' I said, 'Well, I was sleeping.' They said, 'You can't be in here. This is a men-only bunker.'

Hurriedly, I picked up my boots, grabbed my stuff, and went out the door. Blackie met up with me. I was so mad at him! I was constantly mad at him! [Jewel laughs.] I said, 'Blackie, why didn't you tell me no women are allowed in here?' He knew perfectly well, but I guess he didn't know where else I could sleep, so he just figured, 'Oh, we'll just sleep here. It'll be okay.'

Well, it wasn't. They were highly irate, and there were nuns or something that ran the place, and they said, 'There isn't supposed to be women allowed in here!'

I apologized profusely. Anyway, [I know] I'm not going to jail and I'm happy I slept, and I'm out of here.

From there, I don't know if the mission or the thrift store wasn't open yet, where Charlie was, but Blackie, who forever wanted to be in the newspaper, said 'Oh, let's go down to the Clinton newspaper, and we'll talk to them and we'll get in the newspaper.'

So we went down there, and sure enough, Blackie, who is a smooth talker, said, 'I'm Iowa Blackie and this is Minneapolis Jewel. We're riding trains together and we came into Clinton. Why don't you do a story on us?'

They did, and the next day we were in the Clinton paper.

East Coast Charlie and the Thrift Store

Finally, we made it over to the thrift store and there was East Coast Charlie. He was like, 'Where were you? I was waiting for you last night. And I wanted you guys to come and stay in my apartment.'

Well, I knew that was Blackie's mission for that not to happen. His wish was granted; we didn't go to Charlie's apartment. He had to work that whole day at the thrift store.

I went shopping in the thrift store and I found a brown, one-piece… I don't think it was as luxurious as a Carhart, but it was some cheaper version brand that had a zip up overall, and it fit me good…it was maybe five bucks or something. So I had an official outfit to wear while I was riding the trains, which was a good thing because it was still chilly at night and the coveralls worked kind of as batting, to lay down in a boxcar, and keep you from bouncing and hitting the cold metal so much. So I was happy—I got my one-piece suit. And Blackie was happy because we were in the Clinton newspaper the next day. We got our paper and we left town.

Pizza and the Police

We proceeded to take the Chicago Northwestern train, so we caught that out of Clinton, and we were going to Boone, Iowa, which is west of Clinton. Once again, Blackie was familiar with the workers, and one of the workers gave Blackie a $20 bill and said, 'You and Minneapolis Jewel go have supper someplace.'

Blackie knew every eating place. He was basically a vegetarian. He would eat some meat if he had to, but he knew all the salad bars en route from Iowa to Minnesota. He said, 'I know a good pizza place we can go to. We can get vegetarian pizza and eat all the salad we want.'...

We must have been in there for over an hour and a half, and Blackie could eat and eat salad. He was like a bottomless pit. So we ate until he had consumed [she laughs] probably most of the salad in the kitchen. And we still had pizza left over, so we took the box and went.

We were waiting for a train, and I remember we ended up at a car dealership. It was raining again—it must have been the most rain Iowa got during the two weeks I was with him [Blackie]—and the rain came and came, and it was cold, so we went under a semi truck, and the semi truck allows us room enough to sit under there and stay out of the rain. And we had our leftover pizza, too, so that was great. Also, I had a bottle of Southern Comfort I brought with me, because I like to take a little hit here and there and relax. And Blackie was not a drinker, but he did take a hit here or there, I think just to be kind of cordial with me.

We sat under this semi truck and we're relaxing and eating pizza and drinking a little Southern Comfort, and all of a sudden, around the corner police were screeching. I'm thinking, 'Oh, my lord, what did we do? We're not on train property...we just had a couple hits of Southern Comfort each.' I didn't see any law that we were breaking.

Well, the police came out. They ID'd us—they wanted to know what we were doing, who we were, where we were going... As it turned out, this car dealership that we were at had been getting broken into quite a bit, and people were stealing...I don't know if it was just tires they were stealing, or cars, or what mischief they were in, but they had staked out...they had undercover people that were sitting in vehicles across the street from the car dealership, watching. Any kind of activity they saw that didn't look normal, they were to report it.

Sure enough, who are they going to see but these two hobos, like drowned rats, scraggly, carrying our gear, carrying a pizza box, going under one of the semi trucks, so they had to call the authorities and they came to us. We said if they'd just let us go, we'll get off the property and we'd get on railroad property, where we're *really* trespassing [she laughs]. So they were happy with that—after they ID'd us they saw that we weren't criminals and let us go.

Trouble at the Salvation Army

We did catch a train...from the Chicago Northwestern across to Boone, Iowa. It was turning evening again. Blackie had all the answers to where we were going to sleep and what we were going to do. He said, 'I'm going to Salvation Army and talk to them and tell them we need a place to sleep. You wait here.'

He came back about an hour later. He was all happy and said, 'It's all worked out. Salvation Army is going to give us a room to sleep in.'

I said, 'Oh, good.' I thought this will be the first night besides sleeping in boxcars and sleeping in a mission where I wasn't wanted because I was a woman. Maybe I'll get a good night's sleep...

We took our gear, and he said, 'We can't check into the Salvation Army until 7 or 8 at night.'

I said, 'I can deal with that. We can just hang out, walk around the yards, whatever.' We're walking down the street and a car pulls up and an angry man gets out and starts talking to Blackie. I'm wondering what the heck this is all about. What did we do now? And the guy was the...I don't know what you call them...head master guy of the Salvation Army...[She consults with a nearby hobo, who tells her it's brigadier general; another says it's a captain.]

[The captain] says, 'Iowa Blackie.'

Blackie says, 'Yes, that's me.'

He says 'I know who you are. You were just at my place an hour ago. And you said you wanted a room for two men. That looks like a woman to me.'

I'm like, good grief! I had my hair pulled back, and I had my suit on, and it was pulled up so you couldn't see I had a bosom. My face was totally dirty. I had a kerchief on…well, apparently that wasn't good enough. The captain knew I was a woman. He said, 'No, no, no, no. We don't let rooms to couples.'

I pleaded, but the guy said no. He was not going to let me stay in a room with Blackie, tired as I was.

Blackie said, 'Well, what if we were married?'

I said, 'We're not getting married just so we can sleep in a room together! I don't care how tired I am!' So we kept walking down the street. The guy peeled off rubber…like, 'Ha, I stopped that debauchery.'

We ended up back in the yards. I said, 'Blackie, I'm so tired. Can't we just go lay down someplace?' So Blackie and I looked in every boxcar, every grain car, and everything had something wrong with it.

I said, 'The next boxcar that's open, I'll be happy to sleep in it. I don't care what it is.' So we climbed aboard a boxcar, and I don't know what it was—it was all [covered in] white, chalky powder. It's so dumb when I look back, because it could have been something poisonous. It was so fine a powder, I'm sure when we breathed in, we inhaled this stuff. At that point I was so tired, I just said, 'Blackie, I'm going to sleep.' We laid in this white powder and slept all night, and when we woke up we were like ghosts [covered in this white stuff]. We were in Boone, Iowa, and from there we took a train to Des Moines. Blackie knew every single stop in Iowa. Blackie could have wrote his own basic rail guide for Iowa. When we got off, it was raining again.

He said, 'I know this perfect little building we can go rest up.' It was a weird, little brick building that looked like it was built in 1876 for the cowboys to bring their horses in to get hay or something.

Waiting to Catch Out in Des Moines

We kept waiting for a train, waiting for a train. I said, 'OK, Blackie. I'm going across the street to get me a drink.' He didn't like the idea. He didn't drink or smoke, and back then, I would like a drink and I was smoking Old Gold cigarettes. So I went across the street—the train wasn't coming for a while, according to him—and I had a rum and coke and a cigarette and relaxed. There were two guys there that I talked to—no big deal. About a half hour later I came back and oh, Blackie was upset. What was I doing [he wanted to know].

I said 'I ain't married to you. You're not my father. Knock it off!'

He stomped across the street to the bar. He wanted to see what was over there and what was going on. Blackie read them the riot act: 'That's my girlfriend—don't you be talking to her...' He came back across the street and was acting very upset. The train came and we got onboard and headed north, back to Minnesota. He sulked most of the way because I had gone to this bar and had a drink and talked to these two guys. I thought, 'Okay, I don't think I'll travel with this guy anymore.'

Blackie's Mother

Somewhere along the way we stopped in Hampton, or New Hampton, wherever he lived, and we went to his mother's home. Her name was Gertrude. I thought, 'This ought to be a trip and half to see who the mother of Blackie is.'

She was this little farm lady in this little town, and she sold Avon products, and I think I was probably the only female that Blackie ever brought home. She was rather doting on me, and she was very doting on Blackie. Blackie's real name is Richard, and she called him Ricky. She had us go out to the garden—she had a pretty big garden in the backyard with beautiful corn growing and tomatoes, and we picked all this fresh produce. Of course, she knew he was vegetarian, and that was fine with me. She cooked all these plates of homegrown tomatoes and potatoes and corn and fresh green beans. It was a wonderful dinner.

We continued on our journey and arrived back in Minnesota in the yards by the U of Minn, and the train stopped right where we needed to get off, and we got off, and Blackie talked to a few of the yard people. They greeted him by name. We walked out of the yards, no problem with any yard bulls or anything.

One nice thing about Blackie, I thought it was really sweet, he took a piece of cardboard and he folded it in half, and he did drawings of him and me. Of our adventures. The card had drawings of Blackie and I in the rain, under the semi with our pizza box, picking corn out of his mom's garden… a whole kind of plot by plot story line of us.

Iowa Blackie Is Riding the Westbound

I'm still in such a shock. When he died, Linda Hughes, the one that runs the Hobo Museum, called me in February and told me Iowa Blackie died, and I couldn't digest it. 'What did you say again?'

Here was somebody who was a vegetarian. He didn't smoke, he didn't drink. He always carried this weird conglomeration of horrible stuff in his backpack, like bottles of brewer's yeast—icky stuff—I would take a vitamin here and there, but he had all these weird concoctions, and he really watched what he ate. I still couldn't believe it—that he had died—because back in the day 20 years ago, he carried a pack that I swear weighed 200 pounds.

One time when he came into the city, he wanted a ride, and me and C'mon Pat, one of the other hobo queens, said 'We'll give you a ride.' He said, 'You could pick up my backpack and put it in your truck.' Me and Pat – we couldn't even do it, and there was two of us.

I said, 'Blackie, if you don't get rid of some of this crap in your backpack, you're going to end up with a hunchback and a broken back.' I swear to God I don't know how he could carry it, but he did. He picked it up like nothing and put it in the back of my truck. He was really in good shape. So when he died, I couldn't believe it.

Blackie was born in 1948, September 22, and I was born December 12, 1948. When he died this year, he was 62 years old. It was a big, huge shock. Blackie had been coming to Britt here for so many years. His life's ambition was to be a hobo and be a poet and be well-known through Iowa, and he did accomplish that.

TUCK

Tuck was elected King in 2007–2008. He is married to Minneapolis Jewel. Here he talks about why he rode freight trains and gives advice about how to stay safe when riding.

Catching Out for the First Time

I caught my first freight train in 1976. I was 15 years old. I caught my first train in Odessa, Texas. Back then, the oil fields was booming real good. Money everywhere. A lot of work. I worked.

I left home because I felt I was just another mouth to feed, you know, because my mom and dad had separated, and my dad was trying to take care of five kids. So me and my older brother left home. We hitchhiked from Illinois, and we made it all the way out to west Texas hitchhiking. And we decided we wanted to go to California, so we had saved up our money a little bit and we go outside Odessa and we're getting ready to go hitchhiking. And there was this old 'bo under the bridge—I wish I could remember his name— he said 'Where are you boys going?'

We said, "We're going to California." And he said, "Well, that train right over there is going to California." He said, "Go over there to that little store and get you both a jug of water, and go get on that train." And in a little while, it pulled out—it started going.

It was an old piggyback. I never seen another one like it. You might have seen one [*Tuck said to Uncle Freddie, who was sitting next to him*]—not saying that you're old or nothin'. This piggyback is a flat car that they put semi trailers on because it's cheaper to transport them that way—and the railroad is probably making a killing on money. It was hollowed out in the middle. It's like a big ol' bucket down there the length of the car. And we got in there and sat on our sleeping bags and it was so nice. Our heads was a perfect level with the flat of the car where the semi-trailers sits. So we were sitting there, and all you could see of us was our heads poking up from the center of the floor. That was my first train ride, across west Texas, and oh, I was hooked!

That's all it took. I started riding trains and I went all over out through the west. It was just me and my oldest brother at the time. We didn't know what we was doing. We're just a couple of gooby kids. We just kept going west, going west. Then me and my brother separated in San Diego. So I catch a train in San Diego, and go north. I don't have a clue what I'm doing. I wake up, and a young Mexican girl is waking me up, saying "Los Angeles, Los Angeles." And come to find out, there was four Mexicans in this boxcar with me and I didn't even know it. They coulda cut my throat, jackrolled me, threw me out, whatever. I think they was just coming north to go to work...

That's when I first started riding trains. After I got through LA, I met up with these old hobos up in Roseville, California, and they was showing me the ropes. Then there was this other guy. His name was Road Hog also. And he was younger than Road Hog USA. Anyway, he kind of took me under his wing and showed me this and that—how to do this and how to do that.

There's just so many things you gotta know just to stay alive and get where you're going: Little things like, don't put your fingers in the track of the door, don't be catching trains on-the-fly, stay out of the door, don't hang your feet out the boxcar when you're riding because you could hit a switch or another train could be coming by, don't lean on the doors when you're riding because these doors fall off. When you're going down the road and if you're leaning against one of those doors and it falls off, well, you're done.

Just little things like that. Don't crawl under trains when you're crossing in the yard. Go between the knuckles and over the train that way. Just a bunch of things for safety.

A big thing for hobos is being safe. We gotta deal with the freight yard, the train itself; we gotta deal with the bulls, other people who don't like hobos and think we're a bunch of bums. They don't realize that we're a working breed of people. We're not bums. We use that train for transportation.

Like Freddie says, "We work when we want to. We ride when we want to. We sleep when we want to." All that part of it makes it all worthwhile. The dangers are that you gotta sleep with one eye open and you always have a good road dog. That's mine over there.

I got old. I can't do it no more. I got married, got a job. I married the Queen of the Hobos. I met her in Britt, Iowa, in 1994. I chased her for 10 years. She was married when I first met her. Anyway, we got hooked up in 2000, the hundredth anniversary of Britt, and we're getting ready to celebrate our ninth year wedding anniversary this October.

Life is good for me now. I know train-riding life was good. Now I'm trying the other side. Most people do it the other way around. Most people work all their lives and wait until they retire to go ride trains…A lot of these guys that rode trains—they put in 20 years on the job also. All the hobos work, whatever it may be. That's what gets me upset: citizens don't realize we're not a bunch of bums. That's what I'd like people of the world to know—that we're not bums. We travel, we work. We use the train for transportation.

But you got rubber tire hobos, too. That's people that have vehicles that travel around and work also. I used to go to those day labor places—we call them 'rent-a-bum' places, and they always give us the dirtiest jobs nobody else wants to do—the dangerous jobs—and we get our $20 at the end of the day. [He laughs.] Hippity hop to the liquor shop.

IWEGAN AND TUCK

Iwegan, called "Weejun" by the hobos, came up to Jim while he was filming and said he "just wanted to tell a little story."

A Little Story

TUCK: [Introducing Iwegan] This is one of my best friends also. He's the one that got to put the crown onto my head.

IWEGAN: I want to tell you a story about ingenuity, okay? It has to do with a Mexican fellow. We were down in Dalhart, Texas about 15–20 years ago. We had a caboose on private property about 50 feet from the tracks where we stayed. All of a sudden we watched and here come about 20 immigration officers and they had so many illegals they had school buses. They had about 150 illegals. It took about an hour and a half for them to get it done [loading them on the buses]. When they were done, they pulled away with the buses, and the train was there.

And all of a sudden I saw a tree, a scrub brush, he came down the tracks and he found a grainer, which has a hole in it, and he put his little tree legs on the grainer, and he got in and got in the hole. He was a little Mexican and he'd disguised himself as a tree. As soon as they left, the tree caught the train. And I thought that was the craziest stuff I'd ever seen in my life, man. He was about 50 feet in the bushes with all the other trees and they never seen him the whole time.

I thought, he might not even speak a word of English, but he's sharp.

We used to watch Mexicans in the wintertime when it was 20 below zero, and there'd be six of them riding piggybacks in T-shirts. No baggage, and they made it! I got a lot of respect for them.

TUCK: When they showed up in Eugene, Oregon, after coming off that mountain, you'd see them almost frozen to death. How do they do that? I'd die! They're tough! We're spoiled, I guess. We have to have sleeping bags, water jugs, and all that—and tobacco—and them guys can ride with nothing. It's really incredible.

CONNECTICUT SHORTY

Connecticut Shorty and her sister, New York Maggie, are second-generation hobos. Their father, Connecticut Slim, started hoboing about 1928 and married in 1940. Connecticut Shorty was elected Queen in 1992–1993 and took her first ride on a freight in 1993 with Road Hog USA, who was King at that time. When Connecticut Shorty and New York Maggie retired, they became "rubber tire tramps" for 12 years, living and traveling in a 26' motor home they called "Patches."

Two Traveling Hobo Queens

Excerpted from *Connecticut Shorty—Riding the Rails*

Two Hobo Queens, Connecticut Shorty and Minneapolis Jewel, thought "it was about time to add some history to the books" and decided to catch out together on July 16, 1997. After being kicked off the porch of a grainer in Iowa and threatened with jail by a railroad employee, they hitchhiked to La Crosse, Wisconsin, to try a different railroad. They arrived in La Crosse late in the evening, somewhere south of the Burlington Northern Santa Fe (BNSF) Railroad.

We walked for over an hour in the dark looking for the BNSF Yard. We plodded over a large highway bridge that crossed the tracks in the Gillette Street area. This was the third or fourth bridge we had crossed. As we climbed the rise over this latest bridge, our packs, which felt light earlier in the day, now felt like they weighed 100 pounds. In between laughing at ourselves, Jewel and I had several serious conversations, including one about how hard it was to be a hobo. They have to carry all their belongings, acquire food and shelter, fight the elements, make the "carfare," get used to a strange assortment of insects, and put up with frequent harassment from people that cannot understand the lifestyle hobos choose to live.

Jewel suggested we go down a bank, near the bridge we had just crossed, to get closer to the tracks. This sounded like a good idea to me. It was now somewhere around 11 p.m. and the temperature was still close to 90. We started down the steep slope, plotting each step carefully with our flashlights because the weeds were very high. Suddenly, I saw the shadow of a light and exclaimed, "Stop, Jewel! There's a light under the bridge. Someone's down there!" I yelled out, "Tramps walking here, who's there?" (Road Hog USA had taught me to always announce yourself before you enter a camp...) A voice replied, "N.Y. Slim. Who are you?" I responded, "Connecticut Shorty, Minneapolis Jewel is with me." Sounding pleased, Slim responded, "Connecticut Shorty come on down! I've been wanting to meet you."

Jewel and I were still reluctant to go any closer. "Who's with you? How many are down there?" I asked. Slim told me there were four of them and gave me the names of the other three. I was relieved when I heard their names. I had met two of the bo's, Mel and Spotted Elk, a couple of weeks earlier in Staples, Minn., and was pretty sure they wouldn't harm us. As one last "comfort request" I asked that someone I knew come out of the dark where I could physically see them. Spotted Elk, the Indian from Montana, immediately came up the bank to greet us. I was happy to see him again, and Jewel was very pleased to meet him.

Jewel and I jungled up under the bridge, talking with the hobo/ tramps....Eventually, Jewel and I settled in against the bridge abutment, waiting for our train. The bo's had told us exactly what track our train would be arriving on, and there was no question they knew what they were talking about. As we lay resting, but not sleeping, I noticed the air was cooling down nicely, an almost full moon was shining brightly, and clouds were slowly starting to move in from the west. By now it was close to 1 a.m....

At 2 a.m. on July 17th, a mixed BNSF freight rolled in and stopped exactly where the bo's had told us it would....I borrowed a large bucket... to aid us in getting into the open boxcar. We had spotted the open car as the train had come to a stop, and knew that would be our ride. Jewel got in the boxcar, then as I got in, I kicked the bucket away from the train. I was sure Mel would find it when he woke. I staked the boxcar door with a wedge I had carried in my pack and we settled in for the six-hour ride to Minneapolis.

Although it was late night, neither Jewel nor I could sleep. We rode along in the fairly clean, smooth riding car, watching lightning bugs twinkle like thousands of miniature stars, gently lighting up the dark night. A couple of hours into our trip, we rode into an especially fierce thunderstorm. Balls of lightning lit up the entire landscape and streaked across the sky in every direction. We both had an uncomfortable few minutes when we realized we were in a metal boxcar and wondered if they were prone to lightning strikes. We soon forgot our nervousness and began to enjoy the spectacular light show that lasted until daybreak. When the sun rose, several beautiful species of wildflowers added to the glorious scenery along the tracks.

Around 8 a.m. the train approached the Burlington Northern Santa Fe Northtown Rail Yard in Minneapolis…our train was rolling on the third track in. Jewel and I began to feel a little apprehensive, wondering if the train was going to stop in the yard near the K-9 dog patrol we had been hearing about. Then suddenly our train switched to the first outside track and slowly came to a stop. This placed our boxcar around a slight curve, near a bridge abutment, where we spotted a gate opening, in a fence, that led to the road. We quickly grabbed our gear, exited the boxcar and immediately headed off railroad property. Five seconds later our train started rolling again. It had stopped just long enough to let two Hobo Queens disembark safe and sound.

We ARE Going to Ride Your Trains

Excerpted from *Connecticut Shorty—Riding the Rails*
[Note: Paragraphs in italic are my summaries.]

In mid June 1999, my friend Frog invited me to join him on a rail trip from Minneapolis, Minn., west to Whitefish, Mont through the magnificent Rocky Mountains and Glacier National Park. Riding the "highline" with a hobo/tramp who has been on the rails close to thirty years, and was familiar with the route, was better than a dream come true for me.

Our first attempt to "catch out" was on June 22nd in the Burlington Northern Santa Fe (BNSF) Northtown Yard in Minneapolis. Here, along with another friend and seasoned rail rider Preacher Steve, Frog and I sat behind a semi-truck trailer just outside of the yard. We had only been sitting there for a short time when we were surrounded by two railroad bulls and the local police. Our identifications were checked and probably recorded someplace for future reference. We were told emphatically by the head bull we later named "Mr. Nasty" to hit the road. He yelled, "You're not going to ride my trains!"…

[Note: A serial killer named Rafael Resendez-Ramirez had been committing crimes along the southern rail routes, and police were on high alert—Shorty and her friends felt safe traveling the northern routes, but decided they'd go to Staples, MN, to try to catch out, rather than risk getting caught again in Minneapolis. In Staples, they found a two-hole "grainer"—a grain car.]

We threw our gear aboard, each climbed into a hole and in a short time the train was off. The car we chose had a lot of "shake and bake" but we didn't care, we were just happy to finally be on a train. Frog pulled out his little flask of whiskey and we toasted our success.

When we rode through the Dilworth, Minn. Yard we kept real low in our holes. Frog, and another rider he was with, had gotten busted in Dilworth less than two years prior to our trip. Another bust would most likely yield more jail time for Frog and possibly some for me. As we cleared the yard and headed towards Fargo, ND we both breathed a little easier.

[In Fargo, they discovered the train they were on had turned north, which probably meant it was going to Canada. They had to stay in their car to wait out a thunderstorm, and then they got banged around while cars were added to the train. Finally they were able to disembark to look for a train going west. But nothing looked promising.]

[Frog] decided our best bet would be to hitchhike the approximately 170 miles to Minot, ND, and hopefully catch a train heading west there. We slowly walked three and a half miles in the hot, humid 85-degree heat to get to Route 2 west, and put our thumbs out.

After three rides, a check by the North Dakota Highway Patrol and a "Non Citation Field Contact Ticket" from them, we arrived at Devils Lake, ND, still 102 miles from Minot. Frog and I spent a beautiful night in the local park at Devils Lake. We slept on the deck of a recreation building, behind picnic tables, under a four-foot overhang with clear skies and bright stars. The restrooms were open, allowing us to wash up and make coffee (we carry instant coffee in our packs) with our "electric stinger" before leaving the park in the morning. First class accommodations for two hobo/tramps for sure!

[The next morning they hitchhiked again and made it to Minot, where they found the "Sally" (Salvation Army) and got food and hot showers. From Minot, they caught a BNSF train to Havre, Montana. They rode a double-stack container car and crossed the Rocky Mountains through Glacier National Park, arriving in Whitefish, Montana.]

Frog and I passed the time by touring Whitefish, sitting comfortably in the Amtrack Station writing post cards and by taking a nap, on a ledge, under a concrete road bridge that crossed the tracks. The bridge had many signs that other tramps had jungled up on the ledge, and it provided a great view of the rail yard. Around dinner time, Frog scouted the local dumpsters while I watched the gear. He made a good score finding a large package of mostly unspoiled strawberries, a loaf of fairly fresh wheat bread, and a ham and cheese sandwich on soggy bread. We tossed out the soggy bread, for the birds, and transferred the sandwich contents to our new bread. A gourmet feast for sure!

[After staying the night in Whitefish, they found another double-stack container car on a BNSF train heading east.]

Our new ride had only a small well, approximately 10 foot by 20 inches, but it was dry, and since we are two small people, we settled in comfortably as our train started crossing the Rocky Mountains. It was fantastic seeing Glacier National Park in the sunshine. As we crossed the mountains, snaking around multiple curves and climbing steep grades, we had magnificent views of our very long train, with three BNSF Units (locomotives) pulling and two pushing it over the Rockies.

Among the fantastic, awesome, and beautiful things we saw on our trip were: snow on the mountain tops, deer, magnificent waterfalls, the Continental Divide, Glacier Park's Isaac Walton Hotel, tunnels through the mounts, snow sheds (built in the early 1900s), evergreen trees (with a divine fresh smell), prairie dogs, numerous birds, ranches, rafters on the Cut Back River in Montana, horses, cattle, Indian Reservations, and buffalo.

One of the most surprising things I saw in Glacier National Park was Frog's moniker, written in foot and a half high letters, on the wall in a snow shed. He wrote it when he was stuck in the shed for 12 hours in 1984 waiting for a track repair. While waiting, he had a very hair-raising adventure with a black bear. Frog was sitting on a grain car having lunch when a bear came out of nowhere and snatched his bread off the "porch" of the grainer. Acting quickly, Frog tossed the bear the sandwich he was eating, then quickly climbed to the top of the car until the bear left the area. This proves stopped trains in the wilderness can be as dangerous as moving ones.

[Connecticut Shorty and Frog traveled back through North Dakota, toward Minnesota.]

Our destination was the Staples, Minn. Yard, but many of the freight trains bypass it and don't stop in great numbers the way they used to. We thought we might be riding all the way to the Northtown Yard in Minneapolis where we had run into Mr. Nasty a week prior.

The train slowed down in Aldrich, Minn., seven miles west of Staples, but was not slow enough for my comfort level to jump off in the dark on a sloped rail bed. Frog could have gotten off "on the fly" but we were partners on this ride, so we both stayed on the train. A short time later, all of a sudden Frog exclaimed, "We're stopping! We're in Staples! Get off!" We quickly threw our gear off the train and got off. We had ridden almost 2,000 miles and were only a few hundred feet from our final destination, our friend's house in Staples, and we were arriving in plenty of time for their Fourth of July party.

Our fantastic rail trip had come to an end. To Mr. Nasty Bull we say, "We ARE going to ride your trains!"

AFTERWORD
TWENTY-FIRST CENTURY HOBOS

When we first decided to go to Britt, I had no idea what to expect. A hobo convention? What in the world would people do at a hobo convention? And what kind of people would we meet? At the end of the four-day convention—after the memorial service, the ladies' tea, the parade, the election of the King and Queen, the wedding, much conversation, and music and poetry around the campfire—I had my answers. The convention was a window into a culture that most of us know nothing about, and that is why I wrote this book.

Hobos break the stereotype of being "bums." They are intelligent people, highly independent, and very patriotic—it's obvious that they love this country even though many prefer not to "fit in."

They tend to be wary of outsiders, though, especially those of us with video cameras. "You guys always make us look stupid," one hobo said to us early in the convention. Little by little, though, as we started filming and asking questions, they began to trust us, and they talked about their lives, telling us their stories. Several hobos have become friends, and we are still in touch.

Like any group of people, the hobos have their problems. But they also have a strong sense of community. They care about each other, and they look out for each other. Most have had mentors who helped them learn how to survive on the rails. They share what they have, and they pool their money, even if they don't have much, for a common need.

Hoboing has changed over the past century. Hobos no longer "ride the rods," as they did in the early 1900s. Nor are boxcars the preferred way to travel, as they were in the Great Depression. Because boxcars are now made of steel, rather than wood, they are uncomfortable. They are also built higher off the ground, which makes them more difficult to get into. Today, grainers (grain cars) tend to be the car of choice, both for the protection from the elements their construction gives and the platform, or "porch," where a hobo can ride and see the countryside.

The water towers are long gone, having disappeared with the advent of diesel, taking with them the expanse of wood where hobos left messages for each other—"tramp directories," as Jack London called them. These days, hobos still might leave their monikers in train yards and jungles, but they often communicate with each other via cell phone.

Catching out has always been very dangerous—even more so with today's high-speed trains. It is also illegal. Those who get caught risk being arrested, fined, and jailed. In some places, security concerns have made it a felony.

However, hobos still ride. They are, after all, wanderers by choice. And for them, one thing remains the same—the lure of the rails and the freedom it represents.

The traditional group picture of hobos taken every year during the convention. These hobos attended the 2011 National Hobo Convention.

ACKNOWLEDGMENTS

I'd like to thank the following people and organizations who made this book possible:

The hobos who took the time to talk with us and share their stories: Long Lost Lee, Luther the Jet, Tuck, Minneapolis Jewel, Grandpa, M.A.D. Mary, Uncle Freddie, Frog, Iwegan, Connecticut Shorty, and New York Maggie.

All the hobos at Britt, who put up with our cameras and recording equipment and who helped us understand the hobo traditions.

Linda Hughes and the Hobo Museum in Britt, Iowa.

The Salamanca Rail Museum, where I always learn something new.

Stan Carlson, for his wonderful paintings, including the cover for this book.

My writer's group—John Kavouras, Everett Prewitt, and Sarah Wisely—who always question, critique, make suggestions, and improve my books!

The readers of my novel, *Line by Line*, whose enthusiasm for information about hobos made me realize that I needed to write this book.

For More Information

To purchase any of Connecticut Shorty's and New York Maggie's books about their travels, contact them at maggieshorty@aol.com.

About the Salamanca Rail Museum:

In the City of Salamanca, NY, both the Erie RR and the B&O RR had large freight yards and locomotive shop facilities. The Pennsylvania RR also had a line through the city. At one time, more than 5,000 railroaders worked out of Salamanca.

In the late 1970s, a group of B&O retirees started plans for a museum that would celebrate the rich railroad history of the city. There were three stations in the city at that time, but only one was unused. In 1982, Chessie System, the parent company of the B&O, sold the former Buffalo, Rochester, and Pittsburgh Railway station located at the foot of Main St. to the city to house the museum collection. The Salamanca Rail Museum opened to the public in 1984. It displays a large number of exhibits of railroading in the Salamanca area over a century and a half. Railroad memorabilia include lanterns, locks, dining car items, conductors' uniforms, and locomotive items interspersed with photos, historical data, and model railroad displays.

The museum also has three cabooses, an old Erie RR camp car, and two boxcars that are open to the public. The museum is open from April 1 to December 31, Tuesdays through Saturdays from 10:00 a.m. to 5:00 p.m., and Sundays from 12:00 noon to 5:00 p.m. The museum is closed on Mondays. For information, call the museum at (716) 945-3133, or email salarail@verizon.net.

Stan Carlson, Artist:

Stan Carlson is a fourth-generation railroad worker. When he was a boy, his father often took him to the railroad shops to see the locomotives. His exposure to the world of trains led the way to a life of railroading. Stan worked many jobs on the railroad, from track worker to conductor and engineer.

Although railroading was his first love, painting railroad scenes in acrylic quickly became an equal passion. Stan started painting railroad scenes in the mid 1970s, following the techniques of the great railroad illustrators of the 1940s and 1950s. In 2004, an accident ended his railroad career. Stan now volunteers at the Salamanca Rail Museum and continues to enjoy painting scenes of railroading as it was in the golden years. His work can be seen at the museum and on the cover of this book.

Made in the USA
Columbia, SC
09 March 2024